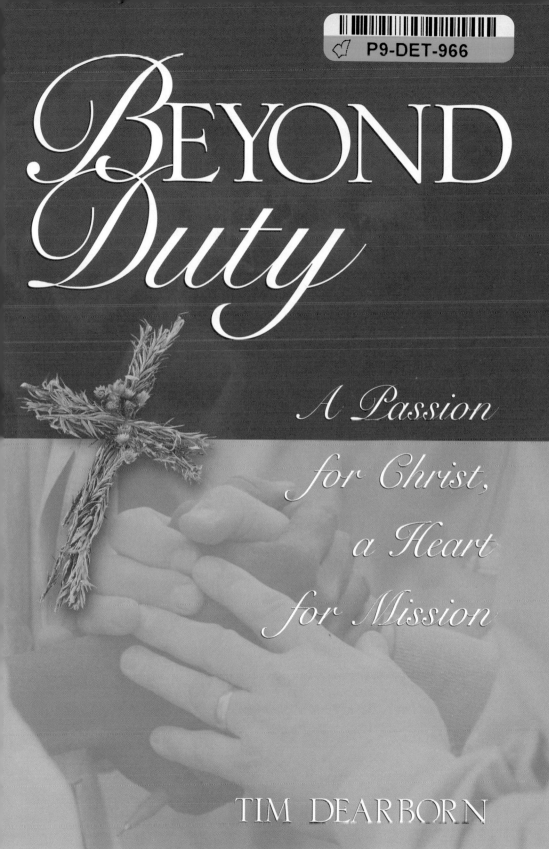

BEYOND Duty

A Passion for Christ, a Heart for Mission

TIM DEARBORN

Beyond Duty
A Passion for Christ, A Heart for Mission
TIM DEARBORN

This book is dedicated to World Vision children around the globe. "For surely I know the plans I have for you, says the Lord, plans for your welfare and not for harm, to give you a future with hope" (Jer. 29:11).

Proceeds from the sale of this book benefit those served by World Vision.

Also by Tim Dearborn:
Taste & See: Awakening Our Spiritual Senses

ISBN 1-887983-04-X

Published by World Vision, Inc., P.O. Box 9716, Federal Way, Washington 98063-9716 and MARC, a division of World Vision International, 800 West Chestnut Avenue, Monrovia, California 91016-3198 USA.

Printed in the United States of America.

MARC a division of World Vision International
800 West Chestnut Avenue
Monrovia, CA 91016-3198, USA

WORLD VISION

Table of Contents

Foreword

Bill Hybels
Senior Pastor, Willow Creek Community Church

More than 20 years ago, my wife, Lynne, and I laid the foundation for Willow Creek Community Church with one mission in mind. With the help of the Holy Spirit, we wanted to turn irreligious people into fully devoted followers of Christ in the context of a loving community church.

As the church grew, the Holy Spirit nudged us to think more strategically about our role in urban and international outreach. We saw God's clear desire that local churches care about what's going on in an unsettled world.

We spoke candidly to one another about the dangers associated with traditional church mission programs. Most of us had come out of churches where there was a high "groan factor" in relation to mission programs. Often, a parachurch group had reached about 5 percent of the congregation, transforming them into mission zealots. Then these new mission converts slathered guilt on the other 95 percent of the congregation, and people gave out of duty.

Willow Creek asked God to show us another way, to allow us to put aside criticism and simply learn from the past. God was faithful, leading us into strong partnerships with leaders who are raised up and trained to work in their own countries. This alleviates language barriers and cross-cultural stumbling blocks that often exist when Americans are placed in foreign countries.

But that was just the beginning of our outreach beyond the walls of Willow Creek. The additional fruit of our labor is that thousands of Willow Creek people caught the vision that mission is more than giving money. They can give their time, their energy, their spiritual gifts and their marketplace expertise.

Now hundreds of our people each year experience cross-cultural ministry as they share their talents and experience with people in need. The less fortunate, however, aren't the only ones who benefit from these efforts. Those who go out to help are changed as well. We've learned that one of the most powerful enhancers of spiritual formation among members of our congregation are these cross-cultural ministry experiences.

So why do we become personally and creatively involved? Not just because the need demands it, but because our hearts require it if we're going to be fully formed and if we're going to have the heart of Christ take full expression in us. Through this unconventional approach to mission, caring for people is no longer a duty—it is a delight.

This book provides you the tools to do the same. Using a foundation of Scripture, Tim Dearborn offers a biblically sound replacement for the duty-bound church mission program. By re-evaluating our assumptions, our priorities and our opportunities, we can all embrace mission with a new freedom and fervor that will change lives—including ours.

As a member of the Board of Directors of World Vision, I am pleased to recommend this book to you. It is my hope that by walking through this study your passion for Christ will grow and your heart will be filled with the desire to serve others as Jesus would do.

What to Expect from this Study

This book is for people who want to know how to be more effectively engaged in God's work in the world. It's for churches wanting to be used by God to make a positive impact on the world for time and for eternity.

But this book is also for people who have come to dread the word "mission," for people who have burned out on all the unquenchable needs that complicate and sometimes devastate our world, and for people who have forgotten or never really understood why they're supposed to care about mission in the first place.

In my experience as a pastor and missionary, I've realized that most Christians find the very idea of mission overwhelming, if not distasteful! My hope is that this study can help you sift through your own perceptions of mission and discover what God really says about the subject in the Bible.

Before launching into our study, let me warn you about what this book is not. It's not a "how-to manual" about "converting" your church to mission. It doesn't provide weapons to be used to coerce and cajole others into commitment to mission. In fact, it's written with what will at first sound like an unusual plea, "Please don't call people to be more committed to mission!"

Mission is not to be the focus of our life and faith. To explain what I mean by this, the first chapter takes the form of the confessions of a recovering mission fanatic: God calls us to a growing commitment to a Person, our Lord Jesus Christ, not a growing commitment to a task, even one as admirable as mission.

From this foundation, we'll move into an exploration of five key themes necessary to a biblical approach to mission. We'll conclude the final chapter with a discussion of a six-point strategy for mobilizing and engaging the Christian community in God's mission in the world—without burning anyone out.

This study guide is intended for use by individuals or groups and is available with a video and leader's guide. The chapters are arranged to offer you new motivation and opportunities to:

- Grow in your relationship with Christ and confidence in God's goodness and reign over earth as our Lord;

- Understand more fully the breadth and depth of God's mission in the world;

- Be carried deeper into the heart of God, into his love for you and for his creation; and,

- Help you clarify specific steps you can take to participate in and celebrate the deep joy and fulfillment of God's divine embrace of the world.

Woven into each chapter are questions for reflection and discussion. You are encouraged to pause at those points, and jot down in a journal some thoughts in response to the questions. Here's the first one:

What specifically do you hope to learn by studying the mission of the church? In other words, this study will be worth it if (you complete the sentence) . . .

Also, at the beginning of each chapter, you'll find an overview of key issues to be covered in that chapter. Be forewarned that many small groups may find more material in a chapter than can be easily covered in one study session. Feel free to divide chapters in half for 12 sessions, or even smaller portions, as best suits your needs.

Finally, remember to pace yourself. The last thing this study should do is add another burden related to mission. Instead, let's get ready to celebrate.

Acknowledgments

A project like this is a team effort. I would like to express thanks to the people who assisted in the editing and production of this book and video series: Kerri Wolcott, Nathalie Overland, Rebecca Russell and Edna Valdez for their editing expertise; Rick Krekel and Robert Coronado for their artwork and layout; Joan Mussa for her outstanding skill with producing videos; and Dwayne Sedig and Mary La Tourelle for their assistance in production. I would like to thank Ron VanderPol for his commitment to World Vision, for his encouragement of the church to integrate evangelism and social transformation and for enabling this series. I wish also to thank Bob Seiple for his friendship and for his leadership within World Vision. Finally, I'm grateful to my wife and family for their persevering encouragement and manifestation to me of God's grace in the Great Adventure of life in his kingdom.

Confessions
of a Recovering
Mission Fanatic

1

Confessions of a Recovering Mission Fanatic

1

Mission lies at the center of God's calling to his people, for it is at the center of his heart for the world. Classic Bible texts verifying this include John 3:16, John 21:15-17 and innumerable others.

From your understanding of these verses and other Scripture, what is mission?

Christian mission is not our arrogant pursuit of other people to make them like us. Rather, it is our participation in God's pursuit of all people to make them like him, and their lives like his. *When we understand this, the relationship between God's people—the church—and mission takes on radical, refreshing new meaning.*

The church of God does not have a mission in the world! The God of mission has a church in the world!

God's church falters from exhaustion because Christians erroneously think that God has given them a mission to perform in the world. Rather, the God of mission has given his church to the world. It is not the church of God that has a mission in the world, but the God of mission who has a church in the world. The church's involvement in mission is its privileged participation in the actions of the triune God. We all know human lives are only transformed by the grace of God, not by human effort. But what does this mean in terms of mission?

Often, as soon as one starts talking about the mission of the church, the focus turns to what we, the people of God, must do. The vocabulary becomes filled with words such as "mandate," "responsibility," "task," "duty," "obligation," "labor." Thus we proclaim phrases like the following:

■ The church must win the world for Christ in this generation.

■ Christians must proclaim the gospel of Christ to all peoples before the year 2000.

■ We must modify our lifestyles to enable a more just distribution of the world's resources, feed the hungry, clothe the naked, build homes for the poor, tear down all barriers that unjustly divide humankind, enable the reduction of the world's arsenals in pursuit of peace, and/or (fill in the blank with your favorite concern_____).

What's more, the church must labor at these demanding tasks until Christ returns.

What are some other words and phrases you often hear used to "motivate" people for mission?

Some suggest that missionary success will be guaranteed if through prayer and spiritual battle we "harness" the power of the Holy Spirit to produce signs and wonders that lead to further expansion of the kingdom of God. While this is a helpful compensation for a primarily human-centered missionary effort, this approach also runs the risk of focusing on what we must do to enable the Spirit to act.

I used to reiterate enthusiastically the oft-repeated phrase, *"The church exists for mission like fire exists for burning."* This idea seemed to vividly encapsulate the urgent centrality of mission for the church.

In what ways might this phrase be inadequate or misleading?

Although I still agree mission is primary and not peripheral, central and not optional if a congregation wishes to walk in the center of God's will, I can't endorse this phrase anymore.

The church does *not* exist for mission. It exists for the Lord Jesus Christ. To set mission before the church as its essential reason for existence is to risk focusing its devotion on an idol. In our age of human-centered pragmatism, where our focus is easily fixed on the fruitfulness of our own labor and where our worth is measured by our successes and failures, we dare not make something we *do* the justification of our existence.

We err if we call people to a commitment to a task. Rather, we call people to commitment to a Person.

Lack of interest in mission is not fundamentally caused by an absence of compassion or commitment, nor by lack of information or exhortation. And lack of interest in mission is not remedied by more shocking statistics, more gruesome stories or more emotionally manipulative commands to obedience. It is best remedied by intensifying people's passion for Christ, so that the passions of his heart become the passions that propel our hearts.

I and countless others like me have erred whenever we've taught people that mission is the purpose for the church's existence. There is only one foundation for a church's existence, and for mission involvement: Jesus Christ. The goal of pastors and mission "fanatics" alike is singular: helping people to grow in their love for Jesus Christ.

Being converted to the mission of the church

During my first few years as a Christian, I was faithfully cared for, fed, affirmed and empowered by a wonderful fellowship of Christians. However, as a university student, my faith was plagued by serious questions. These questions encouraged a secret disdain of mission.

I've come to believe that I'm not alone in this. Many very committed Christians struggle over questions of the apparent arrogance, presumptuousness, imperialism and insensitivity of mission activity. Most of us fear appearing to be intolerant and don't want to risk alienating others through inappropriate imposition of our beliefs and values.

Q What are some questions people commonly raise when they discuss the legitimacy of Christian mission?

I was grateful for my relationship with Jesus Christ and for what God had done for me, but surely the God I'd encountered in Jesus Christ was gracious and loving enough to embrace everyone, regardless of their religious persuasion. The effort of Christians to encourage all people to become Christians seemed to me to be intolerant. I knew that mission was part of our biblical faith, but I couldn't reconcile it with my idea of a loving, accepting God. You might say I was a closet universalist.

I wanted to believe in the Bible as the authority for my faith, but I didn't like the exclusivity it seemed to express. So after university graduation, my wife and I moved across the country so I could launch into two years of graduate study of other religions. My "humble" goal was to prove to myself that for 2,000 years Christians had been wrong in thinking Jesus was the only way to salvation. I hoped to find that Christianity is true for Christians, Islam for Muslims, Hinduism for Hindus, Judaism for Jews and Buddhism for Buddhists. I hoped to discover that behind and above all religions is the same God drawing all people to himself through these diverse means.

Much to my surprise, not to mention my professors' dismay, after two years I concluded I could not, with honesty, claim that all religions point in the same direction. These belief systems' concepts of "God" and of salvation are too radically different from one another and from the God found in the Bible.

For example, a wonderfully inspiring, elderly Hindu professor for two years opened up to me the wonder of Hinduism, then concluded his final lecture saying, "I've tried over the past two years to introduce you to my tradition in all its beauty and splendor. I hope you've found it helpful. All I can say as we end our time together, and as I come near to the end of my life, is that I've pursued God to the best of my ability within the context of my tradition, and I feel so distant from the God whom I've pursued all my life."

The tragedy of his confession and the goodness of the gospel stood in stark contrast. In Jesus Christ, God has reversed the religious pilgrimage. It is not us in pursuit of an elusive God. Rather, God has come in pursuit of us. This is the uniqueness of what God has done in Jesus Christ, demonstrating a love and mercy not encountered in other religions, meant for all the world to know and celebrate.

If asked to summarize in three minutes what's unique about the Christian faith, what would you say?

Mission became the driving passion of my life. I grew preoccupied with how to communicate the gospel of our Lord most effectively. I devoured missionary biographies and deeply admired the zeal of my missionary mentors and friends. But I soon found myself wrestling with a new set of questions that would not go away.

Isn't it wrong to impose our way of life on other cultures?

My problem with mission was no longer theological but methodological. The issue was no longer *should* we be in mission, but rather *how could* we engage in mission without naively imposing our own culture and without tragically destroying the culture of others. We're all familiar with caricatures of the Western mission movement, exporting around the world Western commerce, Western civilization and a Western Christ. I was challenged by these questions: Is it possible for missionaries to enhance the quality of human life rather than diminish it, in order to bring genuinely Good News? How could we best communicate the gospel to people of other cultures without inadvertently imposing our own cultural values that are extraneous to the gospel?

I wanted to understand how we discern what's biblical and what's merely cultural in our faith and behavior. And how do we help others discern the same in their own cultures? Another round of graduate study followed, focused on anthropology and cross-cultural communication. I came to appreciate the rich tapestry of cultures with which God has blessed humankind, and to value our need for the unique insights that can be gained when the gospel is lived out in diverse ways in diverse cultures. I was thoroughly converted to the mission of the church.

Equipped with new tools and understanding, my wife and I were called to Alaska as missionaries. For several years we "tried out" our new-found theories on a community of unsuspecting native Alaskans.

Being converted to the church in mission

In Alaska, I was a chaplain and my wife a teacher on a Christian college campus. There we witnessed a wondrous movement of God's Spirit among the students, drawing many to new life in Christ. It was thrilling to see the power of the gospel change lives, giving students an anchor in the midst of the social and cultural storms battering the lives of Native Americans. However, the air on our campus was a bit spiritually rarefied, and we were constantly confronted with the question of whether this new Christian commitment would be sustained once students returned to the temptations and travail of village life. Would the church be there to welcome these new brothers and sisters in culturally appropriate ways?

Aren't churches too self-absorbed to be useful in mission?

Often congregations are preoccupied with concerns within their four walls. Obviously, this isn't true of you or your church fellowship. Otherwise, you wouldn't be engaging in this study!

But it's sadly true that for many congregations, missionary commitment extends as far as the "blessing for the czar" recorded by the rabbi in the movie *Fiddler on the Roof* : "May the Lord bless and keep the czar . . . far away from us." In other words, "Lord bless all the heathen, and bless our missionaries; but keep them away from us." Visits from missionaries are, for many pastors, mini-crises. Not only do they anticipate a boring slide show, narrated by a dour, dutiful servant who harasses the saints from an archaic soapbox, but they know they may again lose one or more of their most committed parishioners to the "foreign mission field"—lay persons who might otherwise staff church programs, or sacrificially supply more money desperately needed for church budgets.

Isn't mission a peripheral concern for local churches?

Out of self-protection and self-absorption, the church tends to relegate mission to the periphery. We cannot stand to be continually confronted by our inadequacy and continually commanded to do something. beyond our abilities. Further, mission involvement and accompanying rebuffs by the world can reawaken doubts that shatter our conviction that all people need to believe in Christ. We wonder at times whether, if we honestly believed all non-Christians are deprived of salvation, the only option in love would be to be devoted entirely to the challenge of enabling all people to come to Christ. Any other task would pale in significance compared to the eternal urgency of this one.

How do you respond to this nagging question regarding the eternal urgency of evangelism and mission?

If we are unequipped to defend our convictions, we try to shield ourselves from the onslaughts of the world. Our church and Christian friends offer a safe refuge from contact with people who are not Christians. Missionary conferences with dynamic speakers and inspiring stories bolster our confidence that Jesus really is the world's Savior. We give expression to this confidence by supporting others to go out to the world and tell people about Christ.

In their brief times with us, these missionaries must be careful not to open the door too wide, for the chilly winds of the world might blow into the sanctuary, threatening to shatter our carefully patched confidence.

As the church relegates mission—and the world—to the periphery of its concern, the world in turn relegates the church to the periphery of its concern.

Much of the "outside" world views the church as virtually irrelevant and insignificant in the development of global affairs. Though the church is often impressed with itself and consumed by its own activities, the world is basically unimpressed by the church.

We say we believe God is at the center, for "the earth is the Lord's." But for the church to be in the center of what God is doing, the church must become more a leader than follower, more a role model and initiator of justice and mercy, and less a bystander to world events.

When churches come out of hiding and join together as God's people in the world, lives change. Experiencing this reality as a pastor, professor and enabler of people in mission eventually brought me to the staff of World Vision. This organization has the privileged responsibility of partnering with literally thousands of congregations around the world as they participate in the mighty acts of God. In urban slums and rural wastelands, in contexts of abject poverty and awful human conflict, churches are coming out of hiding, joining together and seeing God change lives.

In Spring 1997, Sierra Leone, the world's second poorest nation, experienced a bloody coup. Christian churches there date back to 1785, but at the time of the coup, less than 10 percent of the nation's 4.3 million people claimed to be Christian. What's more, in the city of Freetown, for example, only 34 percent claiming to be Christian attended services at any of 150 churches representing almost 40 denominations. Some 90 percent of the people maintained an animistic worldview. Mixed with this animist tradition was a growing movement toward Islam, which was spreading faster than Christianity among many of Sierra Leone's major ethnic groups.

Prior to the coup, World Vision assisted a group of missionaries and pastors in organizing seven pastors' conferences throughout the country. In many areas, pastors hadn't met together for years because of conflicts dividing them and their churches. At a meeting in Port Loko, 100 percent of the clergy from all area churches attended. Hungry for training and fellowship, the pastors refused to break up the meetings even when insurgent fighting erupted just three miles from the conference site. These pastors remained united and went on to jointly sponsor evangelistic programs.

"A number of 'juju men,' or witch doctors, have admitted that their power is inferior to the power they have seen healing the deaf and crippled," reported Tim Andrews, World Vision's director in Sierra Leone. New converts came forward after the evangelistic programs, filling boxes on a stage with fetishes and charms, or "tie-ties" as they are known locally. In spite of the bloodshed, Andrews wrote, "The church here is so full of hope. It stands in stark contrast to the misery, the war, the hell coming over the radio every day about Sierra Leone."

Years before joining the staff of World Vision, my own view of the missionary significance of local congregations took an abrupt about-face after a tragic experience with one of our students in Alaska. Nathan debated for months whether to give his life to the Lord. He didn't doubt the gospel. Rather, he doubted himself and his own commitment. He feared that after having given his life to Christ, he might "backslide" and dishonor the Lord. Assuring him of God's unfailing faithfulness, we tried to build as much of a foundation as humanly possible into the Christian life of this new brother. Before his return home for Christmas vacation, I even called a pastor in his home town, asking that he look out for Nathan and make an effort to welcome him into local fellowship.

Unfortunately, the pastor never contacted our new brother. On Christmas Eve Nathan fell in with old friends, got drunk and had a fight with his best friend. In the midst of the subsequent row, he accidentally shot and killed his friend's girlfriend. Our entire campus mourned the shocking reality that our new brother in Christ would serve a life prison sentence for homicide. We asked ourselves, "Where was the church? What would have happened if Nathan had been integrated into a Christian fellowship?"

This tragedy was, so to speak, my conversion to the *church* in mission. Yes, God uses specialized ministries like mission organizations, or even Christian colleges, to bring people to Christ. But the kingdom needs local churches ready to embrace people and draw them into their fellowship.

God wants to fill his creation with communities of people who mirror in their human relationships and fellowship the quality of oneness that exists within the very life of the Trinity. Jesus prays, "I ask not only on behalf of these, but also on behalf of those who will believe in me through their word, that they may all be one. As you, Father, are in me and I am in you, may they also be in us, so that the world may believe that you have sent me" *(John 17:20-21)*.

The fruit may be ripe and even harvested, but unless it's brought into the barn it will wither and decay. I was converted not just to the mission of the church, but now to the essential role of the church in mission.

As a result of this "conversion," I became a pastor— appointed to a large, urban American church. I knew God wills that there be congregations passionately participating in his mission of drawing people to himself, and knitting those new believers together into the kingdom community—the body of Christ.

When you think of mission, do you think first of your own local congregation? Why or why not?

I prayed our church would be as concerned about what happened in proverbial Timbuktu as it was concerned about oil for the furnace, carpet for the narthex and teachers for Sunday School. For eight years I watched with amazement as God (often in spite of my well-intentioned efforts) nurtured the creative vision of a strong team of pastors and lay leaders. Mission moved from the church's periphery, as the cherished preoccupation of a few fanatics, into the heart of the congregation's leadership, life and witness. Literally hundreds of people became engaged in mission as the Spirit of God released individuals with dreams and visions so they could manifest "signs" of the coming kingdom. (More about this in chapter 2!)

Being converted to the God of mission

While pastor of this church, I was sent to Haiti to attend a mission organization's board meetings and to meet with national church leaders and missionaries from our congregation. I asked a Haitian pastor my favorite question for national Christians: "What are the qualities of a good missionary?"

Before reading on, and seeing this pastor's response, what would you say are two qualities of a "good" missionary?

The pastor answered without hesitation, "A good missionary is someone who loves Jesus and loves Haitians."

I asked, "How many missionaries do you know in Haiti, and by that definition, how many are good?"

He reflected slightly longer this time, and eventually responded, "I know about 250 missionaries, and probably half a dozen would be good ones."

He quickly explained: "Don't get me wrong. The others probably love Jesus and are trying to learn how to love us Haitians, but the dominant concern they communicate to us is their desire to fulfill their own career ambitions. They are here to teach in our schools, plant churches, provide medical care, enable agricultural reform, train our pastors and encourage economic development. We are grateful for all of this. But it often seems to us that Jesus and Haitians are the means to the fulfillment of these tasks. As long as we cooperate (Jesus and us), everything is fine. But when our ideas or desires differ from their desires, we see very clearly their primary concern: getting the job done!"

As I flew home, I could not get that pastor's comments out of my mind. In a few words, he confirmed much of what I'd experienced visiting missionaries around the world. And I realized I was doing exactly the same thing to my own congregation!

My career objective, my task: making this church as committed to mission as it was to itself. Regardless of how acceptable—even admirable—this objective may have seemed, I was pushing, shoving, manipulating and perhaps motivating members of my congregation to move toward fulfilling this objective. They were the means to an end. Rather than embracing them as beloved children of God, I was emotionally and spiritually coercing them into mission involvement.

In addition, as a church we were reinforcing task-focused behavior in our missionaries. We wanted letters, statistics and reports from them chronicling their "mighty" accomplishments— always expressed, *of course*, as God's mighty accomplishments through them! If we didn't think they were making enough of an impact, we questioned their ongoing viability—and our financial commitment.

This unspoken threat added further pressure on our missionaries to write glowing letters describing their wonderful deeds. In fact, the quarterly prayer letter is a dreaded task for many missionaries. "If I'm honest, I'll lose support" is a common missionary lament.

Yes, fruitfulness is important. However, fruitfulness in God's eyes is first and foremost found in our relationships— not in programs and tasks.

How could you help your church's missionaries feel more free to focus on relationships instead of tasks?

God's passion for people often goes beyond the expected. In our preoccupation with tasks, accomplishments and responsibilities, God's priority is always with relationships. So even when people can't communicate the gospel, God uses other means.

High in the Himalayas, my wife and I met an amazing Nepali woman, who told us of her conversion through a dream. Asleep in bed next to her husband with her children on the floor of their one-room house, this woman dreamed she was being chased by a bull. The bull was her Hindu god, Shiva. Fleeing from her god for her life, she hid in the cleft of a rock. The opening was too small for Shiva, who panted and pawed at the entrance in rage. Then to her increasing horror, the cave started shrinking. Faced with the choice of being crushed by the rock or devoured by her god, she called out in terror, "God of the Christians, save me!"

She had never heard the name of Christ before, but knew of a mission hospital on a neighboring hilltop, staffed by people called "Christians" who worshipped another god. Immediately after her cry, the rock stopped falling, the bull disappeared, and she awoke, panting and covered with sweat. Suddenly, her small home was flooded with light. She rushed to the window to see if some mischievous boy was playing with a flashlight. There was no one to be seen, but the light lingered, and she was very afraid.

Grabbing her coat, she ran through the night to the mission hospital. It was near dawn when she tapped on the door of a Swedish nurse and soon poured out her story. In Nepal at that time, it was illegal both to convert to Christianity and to cause someone to convert. The missionary boldly and simply reassured the woman, saying, "Don't be afraid. You called out to the God of the Christians to save you. He did. The God of the Christians is Jesus and he's the Light of the World. The light in your home was Jesus, giving you his light." Overwhelmed and comforted, the woman returned home in the new light of dawn.

We often focus on the question: "What must we do to obey the Great Commission, make disciples of all nations and hasten the return of our Lord?" This is the wrong beginning point, for it locks us in a human-centered perspective. If we begin with the human-centered orientation, we continually feel constrained by insufficient resources—and the tasks are far greater than we can possibly fulfill.

Biblical priorities reflected again and again in Scripture ask us to begin instead with these questions:

■ Who is the triune God?

■ What is God doing in the world?

■ How are we to participate in God's redemptive purposes?

Mission must never have first place in the church's life. The church is to have but one Lord—one passion—the One in whom all the fullness of God dwells, who has reconciled all things to himself *(Col. 1:19-20)*. If the church today is in need of a conversion, it is always and only to Jesus Christ. We must say an emphatic "No!" to lesser gods who clamor for our allegiance, and a living and joyous "Yes!" to the One in whom all creation is summed up.

This thought summarizes our entire study:
It is insufficient to proclaim that the church of God has a mission in the world. Rather, the God of mission has a church in the world.

Grasp this inversion of subject and object, and participation in God's mission will be a joyous, life-giving privilege.

Miss it, and mission involvement will eventually degenerate into a wearisome, overwhelming duty.

If the church is faithful to the gospel, its focus, passion and delight is always and only Jesus Christ. Once our hearts beat in time with that of our Lord, we can experience a joyously passionate engagement in mission.

Mission's Integrating Theme

2

Mission's Integrating Theme

2

So many conflicting and competing missions cry for our attention. We're so easily drawn and quartered by the pull of divergent needs and calls. If the first key to fruitful involvement in mission is shifting the focus off ourselves and our mission, the second key is finding integrity so that mission involvement may be life-giving rather than life-destroying.

Good News of great joy

Many of us are frequently tempted to mistake busy-ness for devotion, and speed for progress. We lose our joy through frenzied (and often frustrated) activity. Then we wonder why we're so easily divided, distracted and depleted in our mission involvement.

Without a central understanding of the biblical emphasis on the kingdom of God, our terminology becomes one of "I bring you bad news of sad problems."

Efforts to provoke interest in mission are often based on bad news—natural catastrophes, complex humanitarian disasters, unreached people groups, oppressed and exploited minorities, urban or suburban problems and civil wars.

These things are important, but the gospel begins with "I bring you Good News of great joy!"

Woven into the fabric of our Christian faith is Good News! And yet we've made mission the discussion of bad news and unmet needs. Do any of these sound familiar?

- There are 17,000 unreached people groups (or, by other estimates, is it 10,000 or maybe 7,000...?).

- 34,000 children die every day from malnutrition and preventable illnesses.

- More Christians have been killed for their faith in this century than in all others combined.

- Genocide, ethnic cleansing, illiteracy, homelessness, poverty, oppression. The list goes on and on.

Sad news of unsolvable problems

I must confess I once challenged and provoked people into mission using statistics similar to those mentioned above. Good-hearted people responded with compassion and kindness. We worked ourselves into exhaustion with exhortations to give more, do more, be more, care more, serve more, love more, sacrifice more. As fruitful as this could be, something always seemed to be missing.

My church members—including myself—often seemed exhausted. Missionaries we sent seemed overwhelmed by the arduous duty and responsibility on their shoulders.

In what ways might you, or others you know, be experiencing similar kinds of "mission exhaustion"?

Materials written to motivate the church in mission are filled with descriptions of tasks we must perform; responsibilities to carry out; our Lord's commandment and commission to the church; and the desperate needs of the unreached, undernourished and oppressed. And so the church moves out in mission from a sense of duty, obligation and responsibility to attempt these tasks.

Not surprisingly, this commitment to the missionary enterprise of the church produces exhausted servants. The tasks are so great and our resources appear to be so small.

No wonder the church and many organizations' supporters are increasingly disinterested in mission! People cannot handle relentless exposure to catastrophes and crisis. This is not the gospel. The gospel is Good News of great joy!

Yes, we must confront huge problems and fundamental issues—but in the context of a coming kingdom, not in the context of ever-deepening chaos.

I have a friend who works on a disaster response team as a paramedic. He loves his job, not because of the hurt he sees daily, but because of the tangible hope he can offer injured people.

Mission's reward is found when people aren't merely presented with terrible needs, but are given an opportunity to provide tremendous responses. These responses are most powerful when they're personal—giving to real people, not just raw problems.

When Bob Sanders, pastor of Lake Grove Presbyterian Church in Lake Oswego, Oregon, stood before his congregation on Pentecost Sunday a few years ago, he invited his people to contribute enough money to dig one well among the Wolof people of Senegal. A single well could cut child mortality rates in half. It could radically improve an entire region's economy. Bob and a few others from Lake Grove had been invited by World Vision to pray for the Wolof, to study their needs and to send a delegation to visit them. The team had returned deeply moved by the courage and graciousness of the Wolof in the midst of extremely harsh living conditions.

Uncertain what the congregation's response would be, Bob boldly asked for $4,000 that Pentecost Sunday. The congregation didn't give what Bob had asked for. Instead, his people gave approximately $35,000—enough for not one, but nine wells! A growing love affair with the Wolof has since taken Lake Grove members to Senegal many times. The partnership is so meaningful that the people of Badar Gueye, Senegal, have renamed their federation of villages "Lake Grove Land"!

The kingdom of God is Good News of great hope

We are witnesses to great hope, not merely grievous hurt. This should be deeply woven into our psyche as Christians. Scripture tells us, "since we are receiving a kingdom which cannot be shaken, let us give thanks" *(Heb. 12:28).*

Frankly, we don't *really* believe that as Christians. We look at the world and it seems to us that everything is shaken. Everything seems to be teetering on the brink of disaster—and yet the undergirding news in Scripture is that we have a kingdom that cannot be shaken. The author of Hebrews affirms this, saying, *"...we who have taken refuge might be strongly encouraged to seize the hope set before us. We have this hope, a sure and steadfast anchor of the soul" (Heb. 6:18-19)*.

Christ's great victory

If we have this utterly reliable anchor, this certain and steadfast hope, then it is actually blasphemous to focus our missionary communication on descriptions of the great void of unmet (and maybe unmeetable) needs in the world. P.T. Forsyth makes the statement that *"the weakness of much current mission work and much current preaching is that they betray the sense that what is yet to be done is greater than what has already been done . . . the world's gravest need is less than Christ's great victory."* If we understand biblical faith, we will understand that what Christ has already accomplished is far more determinative, significant, complete and important than anything yet to be done.

To what extent is Forsyth's criticism true in your own experience of preaching about mission and other promotion or motivation efforts?

In my work with World Vision and discussions with its leaders, we have begun to recognize that sometimes we've inadequately represented mission in our well-intentioned promotional and fund-raising activities. We've perfected the art of portraying truly heart-rending stories, and providing people with pictures and descriptions of real crises, needs and disasters. God has used our best efforts, though flawed, and his people have responded from compassionate hearts. However, if Forsyth is right—and the Bible is emphatic in its documentation of the truth of his statement—then we must change how we communicate mission opportunities. Instead of relying entirely on presentations of need, we must begin inviting people to participate in God's work by making known to all people the "mighty acts of him who called you out of darkness into his marvelous light" (1 Peter 2:9).

Privileged participation—not exhausted action

Without this news of great hope and full confidence in a completely sovereign God, we will have the sense of mission as an exhausting human enterprise. We'll feel as though we've been given a mandate, a commission and a duty, and that the job is completely up to us. This inevitably leads to burnout.

No one is more tempted to be task-oriented and burned out in Christendom than missionaries. Missionaries relentlessly try to fill the black hole of global disasters and spiritual emptiness and need with the resources of our already busy lives—and it doesn't work.

How do you react to the assertion in this last sentence?

Mission was never intended to be an exhausting human enterprise. Mission is our privileged participation in the life-giving action of the triune God. Jesus invites us to participate in what God is doing in bringing his kingdom. But what does that look like? We all know Matthew 6:33: "Strive first for the kingdom of God." If the kingdom was so central to Jesus' life and ministry, then we cannot afford to be fuzzy about its meaning and significance.

Seeking first the kingdom

Let's take a look at what Scripture says about the kingdom of God.

- The kingdom of God was the subject of Jesus' first sermon when he told the people that the kingdom of God is at hand *(Mark 1:14, Luke 4:18)*.

- The kingdom was also the subject of his last sermon. After the resurrection Jesus appeared to the disciples for 40 more days to teach them (as slow-learning as we are!) what life was all about.

He could have spent that precious time on a multitude of things, but he chose to teach them things concerning the kingdom *(Acts 1:1-8)*.

■ Jesus himself said the kingdom was the goal, the intention and the purpose of all his teaching *(Luke 8:10)*.

■ Even Jesus' miracles were called "signs of the kingdom."

■ In the Sermon on the Mount, Jesus says the kingdom of God is that which we are to seek first *(Matt. 6:33)*, and is to be first among all our prayerful petitions.

■ We all know the Lord's Prayer. Many of us say the following phrase often: "Thy kingdom come, thy will be done."

■ Jesus even goes so far as to say the end of this age will not come until the gospel has been proclaimed to all ethnic groups. All need to understand the Good News of the kingdom *(Matt. 24:14)*.

How would you define the kingdom of God?

Without this integrating vision of the kingdom of God, mission involvement can degenerate into competition among our own programs, ambitions and desires. When the kingdom of God is the goal of all we do, then competing calls and opposing ambitions fade under the sound of the King's marching orders. To engage in mission is to participate in the King's business.

Galatians 2:20 comes to mind: "I have been crucified with Christ; and it is no longer I who live, but it is Christ who lives in me. And the life I now live in the flesh I live by faith in the Son of God, who loved me and gave himself for me."

If I'm to take this seriously then I realize that everything—my words, my deeds, my life—are all signs of the life of Christ. They are ways in which Christ works through me. He is the agent in my words, in my deeds and in my life.

Providing signs of the kingdom

Can you provide a one-sentence definition of your ministry, and that of your church or organization? Let me propose one:

As participants in God's mission, we provide the world with signs of the gospel of hope and the kingdom of God!

Signs of the kingdom can be found around the world, often in surprising places. One day, Simon Ibrahim, an assistant in a Cairo printing shop, asked his garbage collector whether he knew Jesus. A relationship developed, and soon the garbage collector became a brother in Christ. He began to tell others, and insisted that Simon come to the garbage dump to teach them. That was 20 years ago. Ever since, Father Simon Ibrahim has been pastoring the church he and his garbage collector brothers and sisters began—the Coptic Orthodox Church of St. Simon the Tanner (tanning also being a despised profession). This church among the outcast and marginalized garbage collectors of Mokattam is famous for its health clinics, schools, vocational training programs and advocacy efforts for a fair wage for the workers. Out of the refuse of Cairo emerge wonderful signs of the kingdom.

Often we hear people suggest that we are called to bring or establish the kingdom of God. Nowhere in Scripture are we told that we bring, cause or create the kingdom. By the Spirit of God we provide signs of the kingdom. If we use other terms, we are miscommunicating. God brings his kingdom to fruition. He establishes it, not us. God chooses to let us share in his work.

In your experience, how common is the notion that as Christians we "bring" or establish the kingdom?

The weight of building the kingdom doesn't belong on our shoulders, because it has been placed on a better set of shoulders—our Lord's. As soon as we try to shift the responsibility to our own backs, we very quickly tumble under the weight of it. We are called by the Spirit of God to participate with him in building God's kingdom, but the responsibility is his.

This is not merely a semantic issue. These terms mean the difference between something that is life-giving, or something that is death-dealing. We have a pivotal role in the coming kingdom of God. The Spirit of God is sent to manifest signs through us. But the agency is God's.

Jesus' miracles were samples of kingdom life. Because he

chose to limit himself to time and space, he could cast out only a few demons, and feed only a few people miraculously. In comparison to the population of the world at the time, relatively few were privileged to see Jesus in action. Only those living in Palestine and specifically around Galilee had the opportunity to experience a part of what the kingdom was about. But Jesus' reputation began to spread, so that when he came to a new town, people brought the afflicted to him for healing. His kingdom works allowed people to see that their experience was incomplete. In the same way, the late Mother Teresa, for example, cared for only a couple of hundred thousand people in Calcutta, but all 18 million people in that city knew that life could be different because of her example. In fact, her good works have come to be known in the global village and have impacted the world.

As disciples then, everything we do in mission is to be a sign of the kingdom manifested three different ways:

- First, embodied in our lives, as we live lives of grace and joy.

- Second, seen in us through deeds of service and mercy. This part is easy for many of us to understand. A great deal of humanitarian relief and development work is a sign of the kingdom through our deeds. That is what Jesus' miracles were—deeds.

- Finally, signs of the kingdom are to be manifest in our words by prayer and proclamation. Even in places where we are forbidden to proclaim the gospel, we can still pray it, we can still speak words and the Word. Because of prayer, we are never restricted by our words.

Which of these three different kinds of signs of the kingdom do you find regularly in your own life? Your church's? Which signs will you pray that God might increase in your life and your church?

We have the privilege of being living signs of hope—in life, word and deed. But again, the semantic distinction here is that we don't produce the results. We can't make someone else hopeful, or make someone love. We can be used by God to create conditions into which hope might come, but ultimately it is God who produces hope, a fruit of the Spirit, in someone else's life. If the task of producing hope sits on our shoulders, we will feel the constricting band of our own inadequacy and finitude stifling us. But if we recognize that God is the producer of hope, we can breathe again. We are not paralyzed. Then we can become joyous participants in that hope.

The Holy God Loving People Wholly

3

The Holy God Loving People Wholly

3

In this chapter, we will look at:

- *How our view of God's nature determines our view of mission*

- *Our authority for claiming that we participate in a global mission*

- *Christ's comprehensive concern for people's lives*

We've looked at two keys to restoring wholeness in mission:

1. Shifting the burden for the world off our shoulders to the only shoulders able to bear it—the Lord God's.

2. Integrating our understanding of God's purposes in the world around the theme of the kingdom of God.

A few pivotal questions lead us to the next key: Who is this God in whose kingdom we live? And what does God desire for the kingdom's citizens?

The God who is wholly for us

Titus, one of the smallest books in the Bible, provides one of the largest pictures of God:

"When the goodness and loving kindness of God our Savior appeared, he saved us, not because of any works of righteousness that we had done, but according to his mercy, through the water of rebirth and renewal by the Holy Spirit. This Spirit he poured out on us richly through Jesus Christ our Savior, so that, having been justified by his grace, we become heirs according to the hope of eternal life. The saying is sure. I desire that you insist on these things, so that those who have come to believe in God may be careful to devote themselves to good works; these things are excellent and profitable for everyone" *(Titus 3:4-8)*.

Consider what this Scripture is saying:

- A trustworthy statement!

- The kindness of God poured out on us!

- Saved not by our deeds but by God's grace!

- Heirs of hope!

- We can speak confidently about these things!

- Things good and profitable for all people!

What has helped you to discover the kindness of God? How would someone who encountered your church see God's kindness at work?

Sometimes we act as if we have a "holey" God instead of One who is "holy." If our picture of God has holes in it, our engagement in mission will express similar holes. In Christ, God has gone to extremes to show us the extent to which he is "for" humankind. Yet few of us are convinced that God's basic impulse toward us is kindness.

I spent 20 years of my Christian life wrestling with the notion that God's response toward me is as a Teacher. I lived as if God was continually trying to teach me, make me grow, change me. Faced with a choice between something easy and pleasurable, and something hard and challenging, I could be certain the will of God was for the more difficult way. Not pleased with myself, I certainly couldn't believe God was for me. On the heavenly grade sheet, I knew that by grace I "passed," but barely.

The Holy God who is wholly God

A second hole in our theology is the void of confidence that God is indeed Lord. God may be good, but we're honestly not sure he is sovereign. Oh, we say he is, but we live as if a cosmic battle rages between the kingdom of light and the kingdom of darkness, and we're not really sure who is going to win. We act as if the outcome of this battle rests on how hard we pray and, if we are lucky, maybe the help of some angels.

When we're uncertain of God's goodness—and uncertain that he is Lord—we feel burdened and overwhelmed by the needs of our lives and our world. The Holy God is wholly God.

He is wholly for us and wholly Lord. Ephesians tells us that Christ's reign is over all things, not just the spiritual order *(Eph. 1:10, 2:13, 3:6, 3:9-10)*. God is Lord of science just as he is of souls, Lord of the economy of salvation just as he is of the economics of big business.

We can take courage in the fact, as John Calvin said, that "everything is submitted to the kingdom of God, nothing is excluded from it. It is in Christ that all things were created— all things visible and invisible." All things have been created by him and for him *(Col. 1:16)*. He is Lord of everything.

Anglican Bishop Steven Neill summarizes the traditional banner under which the Christian movement has marched, saying, "In Jesus, the one thing that needed to happen has happened in such a way that it need never happen again in the same way. The universe has been reconciled to its God. . . For the human sickness there is one specific remedy, and this is it. There is no other."

This traditional banner is obviously not very "politically correct." What is your reaction to Neill's statement?

This statement only makes sense if indeed the Creator of all Life became one with his creation. The gospel audaciously proclaims that the Holy God became enfleshed on our planet and lived a perfect human life on our behalf. Jesus bore all our darkness, and carried the full consequences of it into life eternal. As Jesus bears our brokenness, we receive the gift of his wholeness.

Since God is wholly Lord, when we encounter his world and his creatures, we are not entering alien territory and facing alien beings. Foes and fiends there will be, but Christ is their only true Lord. Opposition and opponents will rise, but God is their vanquisher. Paul says, "He disarmed the rulers and authorities and made a public example of them, triumphing over them" on the cross *(Col. 2:15)*.

When we move out in mission we are promenading in this procession of victory. We move out to claim the territory for its King. There is nothing pathetic or besieged about the church in mission. We know who is Lord and who has won in triumph. We know who has come to have first place in everything *(Col. 1:18)*. The implications are clear. Christ is Lord of his creation, his church and his mission. When we honestly begin to believe that God is for us, that he is sovereign and that he is Lord over all things, then we will begin to see ourselves and mission as a part of the kingdom of God.

How could we communicate these truths to the many Christians for whom the world seems utterly out of control? They watch the world crumble into chaos, while hanging on until Jesus comes to rescue us.

Living in an age that is increasingly aware of demonic darkness, surrounded by signs of spiritual warfare, it's imperative that we hear again the truth that in Christ we have been rescued "from the power of darkness and transferred to the kingdom of the beloved Son" *(Col. 1:13)*. We *are* redeemed and forgiven—not *if* we try hard enough we *might* possibly be so *(Col. 1:14)*. Creation is not under the dominion of the devil. Rather, by Christ all things were created—both the visible and invisible thrones, dominions, rulers and authorities. "*All* things have been created through him and for him" *(Col. 1:16)*. Furthermore, in Christ the head of the body (the church), *all* things are summed up, united, held together *(Col. 1:17)*. We need to repeat loudly and clearly the joyous song ringing out in the phrase, "*all* things." Christ is sovereign over *all* creation.

A Maasai pastor named David, living in Tanzania, knows this experientially. Rituals to appease spirits of deceased ancestors had been commonplace among his people. Prosperity was believed to flow from the ancestors' blessing, illness and famine from their wrath. David and his church are accustomed to encountering "other" powers and authorities. For example, David recently gathered his elders and their prayers beat against a corrugated metal roof of a mud and dung hut as they pled for the life of an 11-year-old village girl named Esupat. For two days, Esupat had raged through her village, breaking whatever she came in contact with, tearing off an aunt's earlobe, and speaking in the harsh, raspy voice of an old woman. A lump the size of a fist pulsated and throbbed below her collar bone.

David and his elders called out: "We pray that your power will come down to this house, go through every corner, up through the ceiling, and cleanse it. Lord of Lords, we ask that you cast out the demons. We pray for this child who is being assaulted by evil forces. All things are possible through you, Lord. This girl is your creation. We have received wholeness through the blood of Jesus, and hell has been defeated by his resurrection." As they paused in their prayers, the lump on the girl's chest disappeared, visibly, before their eyes. The dazed young girl stood up, stepped outside and was greeted by people's shouts of praise and happiness.

By what authority?

What is the basis of our claims to participate in a mission that asserts authority over all people and all powers? What gives us the right to make such audacious pronouncements? As Christians, we want to appear to the world as loving and accepting. We don't want to be offensive. But in seeking to be sensitive, we face the danger of losing our passion for Christ and his unique identity.

The authority of results

As a result of the worldwide Christian movement, numbering close to a billion adherents today, nearly every person alive has been affected in some way by the gospel of Christ. It influences political, social, economic, scientific and religious perspectives and moral values throughout the world. Many historians unite in recognizing that no other single movement in history has had as great an impact on human life as the one Jesus launched 2,000 years ago.

But critics quickly assail this claim. Too often the church has divided rather than united, destroyed rather than created, and confined rather than liberated. For example, Jomo Kenyatta, former president of Kenya, rebuked Christian missionaries for entering Africa with the idea that everything they encountered was inferior to their superior "Christian" civilization. "They set out to uproot the African, body and soul, from his old customs and beliefs, put him in a class by himself, with all his tribal traditions shattered and his institutions trampled upon. The African, after having been detached from his family and tribe, was expected to follow the white man's religion without question."

The authority of the Bible

Many Christians appeal to the authority of the Bible as the basis for their global mission involvement. The Bible commands the church to make disciples of Christ among people in all nations. True as this rationale may be, it carries limited credibility among people who are not Christians. The world doubts the Bible's authenticity, and further, other religions have an even "higher" view of the inspiration of their scriptures than many Christians have of the Bible. For example, Muslims believe the Qur'an was literally spoken by Allah to Mohammed through the angel Gabriel. Thus Arabic is a holy language and the only language in which the Qur'an can be understood.

The Bible's claims for its own authority are based on Christ's authority. Can you think of ways to communicate Jesus' words so that they point to him, rather than to paper and print?

The authority of love

Others appeal to the authority of love to justify the mission of the church. Love for God and for the world compels them to proclaim Christ to all people. But some would say this is a dubious form of love, calling people out of their traditions and families into social ostracism and rejection in order to obey Christ, and asserting that only Christians will be saved and all others lost eternally.

The scandalous authority

Jesus and his disciples faced this question of authority fairly regularly. The Pharisees demanded of Jesus, and later of his disciples, "By what authority do you do these things?" *(Mark*

11:28, Acts 4:7-10). The crowds marveled that Jesus "teaches as one with authority" *(Matt. 7:29)*. Jesus claimed, "All authority in heaven and on earth has been given to me" *(Matt. 28:18)*, and Paul reiterated this claim by asserting that Jesus is above all principalities and powers, thrones and dominions *(Col. 1:16-17)*.

The sole authority

Ultimately, it's futile to attempt to establish a universally acceptable authority for our claim to a universally authoritative mission. As Lesslie Newbigin says, "The authority of Jesus cannot be validated by reference to some other authority which is already accepted. The naming of his name calls for nothing less than a fresh and radical decision about one's ultimate commitment."

The only authority Christians have for their faith is Christ himself. This authority cannot be justified by appeal to any other authority, for all other authorities are subordinate and secondary to his. His authority is not a derived authority, but the very authority of God himself present in the life of the man Jesus of Nazareth.

Thus the church cannot escape challenges to its claim to participate in a globally authoritative mission. Jesus himself is the only authority we can offer the world. As E. Stanley Jones, a veteran missionary to India, said, "If our faith is real, it is its own protection. If it is not real, then the sooner we find out, the better. There is only one refuge in life and that is in truth and in reality. If our faith can be broken, the sooner it is broken the better. I have taken my faith and have put it out these years before the non-Christian world and have said: 'There it is, brothers, break it, if it can be broken. Only the truth can make me free.'"

How do you react to this bold stance?

God is not an option people can accept or reject and then go on to continue to live normal lives. God is life. Without relationship with God, people cannot experience true life. A leading theologian from India writes, "The whole world is looking for a courageous stand by the church . . . with Jesus Christ as the One absolute revelation, and the Holy Trinity as the one true doctrine of God for all religions and all ideologies."

One can only understand the authority under which the church moves in mission by knowing the Lord of the kingdom. Christ and his kingdom are the singular answer to the world's needs, just as he is the singular authority over all other lesser powers.

The church has, in essence, the same answer to the threat of nuclear war as to family violence; to global poverty as to middle-class financial insolvency; to international terrorism as to personal loneliness: Christ and his kingdom.

We must allow the utter audacity of Jesus' words in John 14:6 to sink down to the roots of our being, and empassion us by their singularly radical invitation to life. "Jesus said to them, I am the way, and the truth, and the life. No one comes to the Father except through me."

In what ways might these words empower and liberate you? Your church?

A group of middle-class teenage Christians at St. John's Anglican Church in Bangalore, India, wanted their faith to make a difference in the world. What could they do? Their pastor, Vinay Samuel, suggested they become involved with some of the tens of thousands of granite quarry workers who with hammers and chisels strained in dozens of quarries surrounding Bangalore. Like indentured slaves, quarry workers rarely earned more than their room and board in the quarry slums. A delegation of youth went to one quarry's owner, asking whether they could provide a school for workers' children. The owner granted permission, but the day the youth returned to begin, he gave the land where the slum-dwellings stood to the local Hindu temple. It's illegal in India to evangelize on temple property. Undaunted, the youth talked with the parents, who agreed their children could come to school—after they had worked all day cutting granite!

I visited this school, taught in candlelight by a quarry worker, with a cluster of tired but eager kids filling the floor, chalkboard slates in hand, eagerly learning to read. Their illiterate parents stood outside, pride in their eyes, hoping their children could escape the poverty enslaving the generations before them.

The youth sought more ways to serve. They found a seldom-used well nearby and paid its owner so workers could draw clean water from it, rather than walk miles to a filthy pond. The quarry owner was happy, because healthier workers meant more granite which meant higher profits. Then the youth found a nurse willing to come weekly and start a clinic. They started a food co-op, buying less expensive food in Bangalore and delivering it weekly to the quarry, bypassing local merchants who exploited transportation-less workers with exorbitant prices.

All this occurred without the youth saying anything about Christ. After all, to do so was illegal. But the workers were filled with questions. "Why are you doing this?" "Why are you so kind?" "No one has ever shown us such love. Why do you?" These were questions to which Jesus is the answer.

Today a church of several hundred quarry workers thrives in that more pleasant slum. The workers have sent evangelists to some surrounding quarries, proclaiming the Good News of the One who has authority over all authorities.

The sole Way to God

Jesus boldly proclaimed, "I am the Way." He did not command us to simply imitate him, or learn from him. He is not merely our guide, example and teacher. Rather, Jesus says, "I am the Way. If you want to have life you must live in and through me."

We live in a world desperately seeking a way to live—a way out of marriage and family problems, financial and social problems, the morass of national and international political crises. The church does not simply offer the world a new set of moral standards and programs to solve these problems. Christianity offers a Person who is the Way. We say to the world unashamedly and passionately, "Consider Jesus. He is the Way." As we walk in Christ, we participate in his perfect human life, and its quality and character is meant to be expressed in our weak, earthen vessels.

The sole Truth

Jesus says, "I am the Truth." God did not choose ultimately to communicate his truth in words, but in the Word—personally.

Truth is not merely a set of correct doctrines, concepts and propositions. Truth is a Person, the Lord Jesus Christ. Jesus has the audacity to say in our relativistic world, "If you want to know the Truth, I am it, I am he." We must not go into our world, which is floundering for lack of knowledge of the Truth, with a set of ideas. Rather, we go with a Person. We don't need to enter into endless debates and disputes. Rather, we invite people who want to know the Truth into a relationship.

I once asked a pastor in India, who remarkably had led more than 400 Hindus to Christ, how he helped people see the truth of the gospel. He replied, "I do that by never saying anything about Hinduism. Rather, I say to people, 'Have you considered Jesus? He is the Truth and he will set you free.'"

The sole Life

Jesus says, "I am the Life." Jesus did not merely spiritualize human existence, concerning himself only with people's souls and spiritual destiny. He robustly demonstrated concern for all of people's lives, for he is Life.

He invites people to life when he calls people to himself. Life uninhibited by greed and injustice, illness and oppression, fear and powerlessness, sin and darkness. Jesus says to the world, "Come to me, all you that are weary and are carrying heavy burdens, and I will give you rest. Take my yoke upon you, and learn from me; for I am gentle and humble in heart, and you will find rest for your souls. For my yoke is easy, and my burden is light" *(Matt. 11:28-30)*.

Jesus says to the world, "I have come that they might have life and have it abundantly" *(John 10:10)*. We do not go to the world with life as an all too vulnerable possession that must be defended. Rather, we go in the Person who is Life and who has triumphed over all that can possibly attempt to inhibit people from experiencing life's fullness.

Speaking from the land of religious pluralism—India—Bishop Osthathios from the Mar Thomas Church said, "Is Jesus Christ so weak that we have to defend him? . . . Does he not have a uniqueness of his own which will ultimately triumph by virtue of its own strength? . . . Are we not courageous enough to believe that Jesus Christ is the Way, the

Truth and the Life for all humanity and all religions and ideologies and that truth will ultimately triumph owing to its intrinsic value?"

No More Ghosts and Corpses: The Beginning of People in Community

4

No More Ghosts and Corpses: The Beginning of People in Community

4

The God who saves souls?

How often have you heard the phrase "saving souls"? Is God primarily concerned with our souls?

A soul is a spirit without a body. Some would say such a being is a ghost. Is God in the business of saving ghosts?

We all know the command to love the Lord with all our hearts, souls, strength and minds, and to love our neighbors as ourselves *(Mark 12:28-34)*. Loving God in this manner means to love him with our whole person, not just with our souls.

Soul-saving churches that engage only in evangelism, seeking to convert souls while leaving the rest of people's lives unchanged, are really only relating to ghosts, souls without bodies. Churches passionately pursuing social justice and welfare, but unwilling to call people to repentant faith in Jesus Christ, are really only caring for corpses, for a corpse is a body without a soul. Both circumstances make a mockery of the gospel of God's kingdom and his reign over bodies and souls, now and forevermore.

For decades, Christian leaders have debated the meaning of this command. Is it a higher priority to engage in evangelism or development, to "save souls" or feed the hungry? Instead of bringing God's reign to bear on the whole of life, to make lives whole, the church often oscillates between preoccupation with ghosts or corpses, rather than people.

At the International Congress on World Evangelization in 1974 in Lausanne, Switzerland, delegates from throughout the world agreed: "The evangel is God's Good News in Jesus

Christ; it is Good News of the reign he proclaimed and embodies; of God's mission of love to restore the world to wholeness through the Cross of Christ and him alone; . . . It is Good News of liberation, of restoration, of wholeness and of salvation that is personal, social, global and cosmic."

If we live out a biblical faith, we'll engage in ministries and send missionaries that extend both hands of the gospel: the hand inviting individuals to repentance, faith and eternal reconciliation with God through Christ Jesus—and the hand embracing others' physical and emotional well-being, the hand of social justice, mercy and compassion, embodying the goodness of God's kingdom on earth. One is not a means to the other, for both are equally significant to life in the eternal kingdom as described by Scripture.

What is your reaction to this idea of churches erroneously focusing on "ghosts" or "corpses"—souls or bodies? How do you respond to the question, "If our ultimate destination is heaven, what difference does it make what happens to our bodies, our physical lives here and now?"

The God of saints who serve

The God who saves persons, not just souls or bodies, is the God who calls us personally, by name. Paul begins many of his epistles with the greeting "from Paul, a servant of Jesus Christ, to all the saints" at Colosse or Philippi or Ephesus *(Col. 1:2; Phil. 1:1; Eph. 1:1)*. What would happen in our relationships if we honestly viewed ourselves and those in our fellowship as saints? We relegate saints to stained glass and legends about church heroes. We think, "Only the exceptional among God's people could possibly be saints." No! If we take the gospel seriously, we are saints! In receiving God's grace and peace, in being forgiven and redeemed, we are restored to the fullness of God's image in Jesus Christ.

We've been set apart for a special purpose: to embody the fruitfulness of the kingdom of God in all we do. This is not just the calling of an extraordinary few among the faithful. Sainthood is for the commonplace Christian.

*What are the implications of this two-fold identity:
servant and saint? Which identity is easier for you to
grasp for yourself? Why?*

When we gossip or otherwise hurt people, they may well be saints we are wounding, saints we criticize, saints we compete against. What would happen to our own self-perception—let alone our perception of others—if every morning in the bathroom mirror, we greeted ourselves as "Saint Timothy or Mary or Robert or Brenda"? Saints!

I once spoke about this in a class on spiritual disciplines, suggesting that those who could not "fast" from food could fast from gossip or self-criticism or lying. Fasting is a discipline by which we lay aside our addictions so we might run more swiftly into God's gracious arms. The next week, an elderly member of the class announced, "I had the best week of my entire life. I've chronically criticized myself, continually reminding myself what a failure I was. This week I abandoned all that, proclaiming to myself in the mirror every morning that because of the grace of God, I am a saint, a creature of immeasurable worth. It worked. I've felt new life, and a new capacity to care for others."

When we recognize our status as saints, we are freed to be one another's advocates, cheering one another on in the pilgrimage of faith—rather than accusers, caustically identifying perceived deficiencies of faith and obedience. We are no longer imprisoned in our disabilities, but discover instead the truth that God's strength is made perfect in our weakness *(2 Cor. 12:9)*. Confrontations with the brokenness of the world or our own inadequacies no longer require a defensive response, but become opportunities to receive more fully the sufficiency of God's grace.

Grace, an appropriately named woman in our church, came to Christ on Christmas Eve at a Salvation Army Hall, while her motorcycle-gang-leader-lover was robbing a bank and killing its guard. She wryly comments that her new life in Christ and her prison ministry began the same night. Over the next decades, Grace became notorious in Seattle, not as a gang member, but as a person with audacious boldness.

A black belt in karate, Grace went where few others dared. She carried a note in her purse: "Dear purse snatcher. I'm sorry that life has brought you to the point that you must steal for your habit. Help yourself to my money, but it'll probably only help you for a few moments. I wish you'd return my purse and driver's license. It's such a bother to replace them. But beyond giving you my money, which will help for only a few seconds, I'd like to give you my Lord who'll help you for eternity. Here's my phone number. I'm usually home after 11 p.m."

Grace led dozens of pursesnatchers to Christ. She was so notorious that once, after her purse was stolen, the thief sneaked back up to her, shamefaced, returning her purse. "I'm sorry," he said. "I didn't realize whose purse I was taking."

Grace was equally famous for her "School for Prostitutes." Concerned for the future of dozens of women of the night she led to the Lord of Light, she started a school to teach them a new life. Enrollment requirements included faith in Christ, desire for a new vocation and permission from their pimps. She's told many hair-raising stories of boldly going to prostitutes' pimps, requesting the "release" of "their" women for a new life in Christ. She was never turned down.

God's strength is made perfect in ordinary saints who are determined to bring grace to the streets.

Who is someone you could "cheer on" in their life as a saint? How?

Extending both hands of the gospel

When I served as missions pastor of University Presbyterian Church in Seattle, our church leadership believed all members of our congregation were gifted and called as serving saints. With this in mind, we invited everyone to make a prayerfully-informed commitment to express Christ's love in one tangible way to our city over the course of a summer. A Young Life club for youth with cerebral palsy began; a women's group started writing weekly congratulations cards to new parents who announced births in the newspaper; two women began building sandwiches for a street mission (now amounting to tens of thousands of sandwiches); our church choir sang public concerts in the park; Bible study lunches began in office buildings; the list goes on and on. Mission moved from the hands of the fanatical few to the center of the life of our church.

Not the God of the sacred or the secular, but the God of everything!

Jesus worked within all aspects of his own society, both the sacred and the secular. Jesus was not politically neutral, refusing to take a position regarding society. His condemnation as a revolutionary criminal by all the existing powers indicated that he was anything but a guardian of the established order.

We often think of Jesus' authority over the spiritual realm. He told demons to flee, he was ministered to by angels and he spoke with authority on spiritual matters. But in Matthew 28:18-20, Jesus says, "*All* authority in heaven and earth has been given to me. Go therefore and make disciples of all nations, baptizing them in the name of the Father and of the Son and of the Holy Spirit, and teaching them to obey everything that I've commanded. And remember, I am with you always, even to the end of the age."

This statement conveys not only spiritual implications, but political, cultural and social implications as well. When Jesus said all authority was given to him, he did not mean the sacred and not the secular. He meant *everything*. Total authority. "*All* authority in heaven and on earth." Authority over kings, governments, earthquakes and gravity. A first-century listener could not have heard him without being challenged by the radical political and social implications of his teaching.

Jesus also claims cultural authority when he commands that disciples be made of all ethnic groups *(Matt. 28:18-20)*. God knows our approaches to life are determined far more by our ethnicity than by our nationhood. There may be 235 nations in the world today, but the words Jesus chose were "all ethnic groups." He realized one's ethnicity didn't change according to the political lines drawn and redrawn throughout history.

Regarding social authority, Jesus told his disciples to teach others to observe all his commands. If we are to obey his commands, what are his commands? What did he spend his time teaching about? Many of Jesus' teachings pertain to money, sexuality and social relationships. Our natural tendency has been to compartmentalize Jesus' teachings as strictly spiritual statements. Yet his teachings were complete. We're not just called to obey his spiritual authority, but his political, cultural and social authority as well.

What issues does this raise for you? For your church?

I recently taught a seminary course on Christian ethics, and a student who'd studied with me a few years earlier came to visit. He said, "God used your class to 'convert' my pocketbook. My whole approach to money changed. Last year I took another class that 'converted' my marriage. I live my family life totally differently because of it. This year I've come to take a class I hope will 'convert' my use of the natural environment." I believe Jesus is pleased with this man's conversions!

News that Jesus possesses *all* authority, authority over *all* of life, brings needed relief to pastors, congregational boards, missionaries and to all believers, who can then rest in the confidence that we are not competing for our share of available meager resources—whether money, time or talent. Pastors do not compete with missionary recruiters for personnel. Mission committees do not compete with other elders for a larger piece of the church fiscal pie. We can all receive enough to do what God calls us to do.

Paul speaks of this in Colossians, claiming that the gospel is bearing fruit and increasing in *all* the world *(1:6)*; asking that those he prays for would be *filled* with the knowledge of God's will *(1:9)*; and that they would walk worthily, fruitfully, powerfully, joyously and thankfully *(1:10-12)*. God frees us to live and love in the Spirit *(1:8)*, empowering us to bear fruit in *every* good work, *increasing* in the knowledge of God *(1:10)*. God strengthens us with his *glorious might (1:11)*. We are not merely patient, but enabled to attain all steadfastness and patience.

In the midst of our chronically dissatisfied generation, in which few ever feel they have enough of anything, in which our cups are typically viewed as more than half-empty, are Paul's words mere spiritualized hyperbole?

When Paul speaks of being strengthened by the Holy Spirit in Ephesians 3:16, he employs the strongest possible words, praying that we be "made mighty" with power through the Holy Spirit. When he says, "In any and all circumstances I have learned the secret of being well-fed and of going hungry, of having plenty and of being in need. I can do all things through him who strengthens me" *(Phil. 4:12-13)*, he literally says every circumstance, and *all* things! *This* is the abundant life Christ gives *(John 10:10)*, pressed down, running over, abounding.

What implications for your own life and for your church's ministry can you find in Scripture's assertion that Jesus holds spiritual, political, cultural and social authority over all things?

God's redemptive totalitarianism

Veteran missionary E. Stanley Jones described Christ's approach to society as "God's redemptive totalitarianism." God's redemption of his creation, his people and the whole kingdom in total imply that the Christian life is more than an individual, spiritual relationship. Through our relationship with God in Christ, we're called to participate in the transformation of our economic, political, social and environmental relationships as well. Without this *whole* kingdom, people remain only partly converted.

Our churches are filled with people who are partly converted—their souls may be converted, but their sexuality or bank account isn't. Do you have a theology of money, of recycling, of government? Does God? If we really believe, as the psalmist tells us, that the earth is the Lord's and the fullness thereof, then our theology must apply to the entire world, not just parts of it. If we confine our faith to "spiritual" concerns, we erroneously reinterpret and spiritualize the vast socioeconomic and political teaching of Scripture. We also deprive ourselves of biblical guidance for practical, daily aspects of our lives, leaving us likely to resolve our daily earthly concerns by the values of this world rather than those of God's kingdom.

Most people's normal view of the world is divided into two kingdoms. The kingdom of God includes the church, the spiritual and the sacred. The kingdom of this world is the realm of finance, politics, economics and nature. God may be Lord of our Sundays and devotional times, but the earthborn totalitarianisms—socialism, materialism, capitalism, narcissism, socialism, humanism or whatever "ism" is in vogue—dominate our daily existence if God is not the Redeemer of all of our lives.

One way or another, all of humankind falls subject to totalitarianism. The "isms" of this world ultimately diminish and destroy life. Or "God's redemptive totalitarianism" redeems and fulfills human existence within an eternally harmonized creation.

We must remain clear, however, that redemptive totalitarianism is God's, not that of the church, the state or our own egos. Non-redemptive, earthborn totalitarianisms are what we see in religious fundamentalist movements. Whenever we see humans seeking power to rule over others, then we have another earthborn "ism"—whether it's in the name of God, the church or a cause. Scripture recognizes that God's redemption of all creation is only in part now. God's intention is that it be in total, but we live for the time being in the "now" and the "not yet."

The Spirit of God desires that we be living signs of the kingdom, to provide visual aids of what life will look like one day when the kingdom is here fully. We will not bring the kingdom or build the kingdom, but our privilege is to live out previews of "coming attractions," revealing what this kingdom will look like.

Beyond Duty to Delight: Celebrating a Joyous Adventure

5

Beyond Duty to Delight: Celebrating a Joyous Adventure

5

In this chapter,
we will look at:

■ *How to move
beyond duty
and obligation*

■ *How to cope
with the
sorrow,
sacrifice and
suffering
that often
accompany
participation
in mission*

■ *How to live
in Christ's
triumph*

We've explored four keys to involvement in mission:

1. Recognizing that it is God's mission—not ours.
2. Understanding the kingdom of God as the crux of God's purposes in the world.
3. Affirming the full wonder of who God is and all that God has done in Christ.
4. Embracing God's redemption of every aspect of our lives.

These truths can have a profoundly freeing impact on our lives. Participation in God's mission is not a somber duty. It's a joyous privilege and adventure. This is the fifth key—being set free to celebrate our role in God's mission.

Loving God with our whole hearts

What would you think of a friend's marriage if he said to you, "I'm sorry to bother you. I'm sure you'll find this offensive, or at least boring. I feel very embarrassed talking about this, but it's my duty and responsibility and therefore I must. It will only take me a few minutes. Do you mind if I say something? . . . It's my duty as a good husband to tell you what a wonderful wife I have. She's exceptionally kind and I love her."

You wouldn't be very impressed, would you? You might even question the quality of the marriage. Yet this is precisely what we do with the Lord God. We move out into the world feeling awkward and embarrassed, motivated by duty, discipline, commitment and obligation. William Carey titled his premier 1792 motivational tract on mission "An Enquiry into the Obligations of Christians to use Means for the

Conversion of the Heathens." I don't mean to question the zeal or devotion of William Carey. His works were dynamically used to motivate the church of his time for mission. I do, however, question the appropriateness of the theme of duty and obligation that so often dominates discussions of mission.

When have you felt most free to talk with someone about Christ? Why? What helped you feel natural and at ease?

What happened to the love affair? A young man or woman who has just fallen in love can't wait to tell others the great news. It's not a duty or responsibility. Lovers post it on billboards, carve it into trees, fly it behind planes at football games for all the world to see. C.S. Lewis made this striking comment, "Duty is the cast which we put around broken love."

The only point of doing something out of duty should be to let love heal. Duty is only a temporary fix. Unfortunately, the mission movement seems encased in a permanent cast or plaster of obligation. I'm ready to call for a moratorium on all duty and task language. I don't love my wife and my children because it is my obligation, duty and responsibility to love them. That motivation would turn them into a project, and no one likes to be someone else's project. I love my family because it is my privilege and it brings me great joy. So it is with participating in the mission of the God of love.

A joyous love affair

As Christ's followers, we've been wooed into a love affair—that of the Creator of the cosmos with his rebellious human creation. Love is not adequately expressed in the language of "duties, oughts, responsibilities or musts." Love language is always a language of joy. However, love language does have room in its vocabulary for sacrifice, sorrow and even suffering. All parents know the decision to have children is accompanied by the decision to wear our hearts on the outside of our bodies for the rest of our lives. Love includes the vulnerability caused by entering into others' lives—and allowing them permanent entrance into our own.

During his last sermon on earth, Jesus let us in on an astonishing secret. After his resurrection, he spent 40 days with his disciples, giving them his last instructions. We hear some of the dialogue in Acts 1. The disciples were still trying to get God to be their servant, asking, "Is now the time that you will restore the kingdom to Israel?" In effect, they were saying: "Jesus, your miracles were marvelous. Your teaching was outstanding. Your denunciation of the authorities was scandalous. Your crucifixion was terrifying. Your resurrection was awe-inspiring. We've followed you for three years, trying to obey your commands. Now we've got just one request. Will you do something for us? All we want is for Israel to be restored to its power and grandeur among the nations, and for us to rule on those thrones you promised."

This has often been the question the church has asked its Lord. "Will you please serve us, O Lord? Will you please provide for us in the way we'd like to be provided for?"

What are some examples of this common religious impulse to make God our servant?

Jesus' response is staggering: "It's not for you to know the timing of the fulfillment of the Father's purposes. However, you need to know something. You're going to be my witnesses." That sounds innocent enough, until we realize the word Jesus chose for "witness." *Marturia* is the same word from which we get the word "martyr." I wish Jesus would have used some of his other linguistic options. In 2 Corinthians 5:20, Paul refers to us as ambassadors. I like that. "Ambassador" conjures up images of flags waving, limousines racing, sirens blaring and people respectfully moving out of the way. Status and dignity. If that's too noble, he could have said, "You will be my spokespersons, or representatives." Anything but martyrs!

In modern English we tend to think of a martyr as someone who is already dead. In a very real sense, that's true of us. After all, we have been crucified with Christ, so it's no longer we who live but Christ who lives in us *(Gal. 2:20)*. I don't think that was Jesus' point, however. A martyr is somebody who witnesses with her life, one who lays down her life for what she believes. We are called to witness with our very being, in our words, our life and our deeds.

Q What's your reaction to this notion that to be a witness of Christ is to be a martyr? Other than dying, what are examples of ways we "lay our lives down" as witnesses?

The joy of broken hearts

Several decades before coming to work for World Vision, my understanding of the Christian faith and of mission was profoundly influenced by one of the most famous phrases of World Vision's founder, Bob Pierce: "Let my heart be broken with the things that break the heart of God." When we love someone, we become interested in what interests them. Loving God means sharing in his love for the world.

When a congregation is disinterested in mission, the roots of its malady are fundamentally spiritual. The remedy is conversion, not to a cause or task, but to a Person, the Person who is Lord of creation. When one gives one's life to the Lord, one shares the Lord's concerns, participating in his love for what he has made and redeemed. If we love Christ, we love and want Christ's best for those whom he loves. It's as simple as that. Mission is nothing more and nothing less than a love affair.

I remember standing on a street corner in Calcutta, after having spent a week on the streets of that hellish city trying to understand life there. I watched a family emerge from their shack built out of refuse, precariously balanced against a wall, dangerously close to adjacent traffic. Finally I'd seen more than I could take. Weeping, I wondered what I would do if that family was actually my family, if they were my brothers and nieces struggling to survive. I wouldn't be able to walk sadly away. At that point, the Lord said, "They are your brothers and nieces, for they're beloved children of mine."

To my Eskimo friend, Nathan—the student I mentioned in the first chapter who came to Christ and a few weeks later accidentally killed his best friend's girlfriend—this could all sound like a fairy tale as he sat in his prison cell. Condemning himself for the horror of his actions, Nathan refused to accept any contact with his Christian friends. Our letters were returned. Each one inadvertently stabbed him as an indictment of his sin. One day, a high school church youth group visited his cell block, singing and giving testimonies to the new life they'd found in Christ. Nathan fled to the rear of his cell, covering his head with a pillow to drown out their guilt-inducing reminders.

One student came to the bars of his cell, and said, "God loves you."

Nathan uttered a muffled, "Go away. I don't want to hear that."

The student persisted, "There's nothing you could do to make God stop loving you."

Nathan rose up and said, "God could never love me after what I've done." The student listened while Nathan poured out his story: his conversion to Christ, his fight and his accidental act of murder.

Once again the high school student reiterated the Good News, "God will always welcome us back home when we say we're sorry and return to Christ."

Tearfully, the two eventually knelt on either side of the bars, and Nathan poured out his heart to his waiting Father.

I often wonder where Nathan would be today if that youth group hadn't penetrated the walls of his prison. Did that high school student share Christ with Nathan out of duty, as a painful act of obedience to God's command? Was that student's life changed, along with Nathan's?

Pray for individuals you know who need to hear, "Nothing you could do would make God stop loving you." How could you stand outside the bars of their life and help them know this?

Embracing the passion of mission

In a culture that succeeds in many ways at insulating us from suffering and pain, the hazards of missionary service can pose a daunting obstacle. Who consciously chooses awkwardness, inconvenience, embarrassment and even risk? As I write this, one of our daughters is in Siberia and another in Uganda. Both chose to serve those at risk—deaf children in Siberia and AIDS orphans in Uganda—and in so doing put themselves at risk. Why take chances with one's own health, security and emotional contentment? The answer is simple. We long for others to know the security found in Christ's kingdom.

Our daughter in Uganda found the confirmation of this answer in the face of Annet, the 7-year-old girl in Uganda whom we sponsor through World Vision. Her father died from AIDS when she was only a few months old. Her mother has not been home for the past year, as she now is on her death bed. Annet and her twin sister are probably both HIV positive, but then no one tests for it in her region in Uganda. It's almost assumed. When the translator told her that Andrea's family was her sponsor, joy filled her eyes. She grasped Andrea by the hand and said, "Then your father is my father, and we're sisters."

Years ago my wife and I had the privilege, with Bruce and Hazel Larson (at the time, Bruce was senior pastor at University Presbyterian Church in Seattle), of taking a group from our church on a pilgrimage to China shortly after that country was opened to tourists. We informed the tourist officials that we were a Christian group and wanted to learn as much about the church in China as possible. They obliged, and many extraordinary encounters followed. A woman we met in Beijing was one of the first woman pediatricians in China. During the Cultural Revolution, she'd been doubly disdained—first for being highly educated, second for being a Christian. For three years she was assigned the humiliating task of sweeping streets in a rural village, in spite of the obvious need for pediatricians. Her job performance outraged her keepers. Not only did she sweep the streets thoroughly, she did it joyously.

She gleefully recounted a conversation with her guards, when in exasperation they asked, "Why are you so happy? You, a mighty doctor, should feel utterly humiliated. You're nothing but a dunce cap-wearing street sweeper."

She answered, "I can sweep streets for the glory of God and the good of my country, or I can take care of God and my country's children. Either way, it is to God's glory. You choose how I might serve."

Might this be what Paul means when he says, "For I decided to know nothing among you but Jesus Christ and him crucified" *(1 Cor. 2:2)*? This woman didn't serve in lonely, isolated suffering. She served with her crucified and risen Lord. We asked a Chinese pastor who'd been imprisoned for three years whether he had any word he'd like us to take back to our church. He answered, "Tell them God is faithful. He can be trusted."

Christians have only one answer to the horrific problem of suffering: Christ crucified—Christ who bore, participates in and redeems our pain. Paul is saying his motive, goal and ambition in ministry was to know Christ crucified.

- Not only Christ in his resurrected glory, but Christ in his crucified pain.
- Not Christ in singular isolation, but Christ among the people he was serving; Christ dying for their sins.
- Christ bearing people's pain and suffering.
- Christ present as the light of their darkness.
- Christ delivering them from a doubt-filled existence.

When we are equipped with a biblical theology of passion, we can embrace suffering because it is no longer senseless. On the Cross it has been redeemed and made productive. Further, we no longer suffer in solitude. God is no stranger to sorrow. Through whatever pain we encounter, we participate in the life of our Lord at his moment of deepest agony, and we experience our solidarity with Christ's people when we share in their suffering. This empowers and propels us to enter into the suffering of others, finding there the presence of our crucified and risen Lord.

The wonder of the gospel and the ultimate impetus to Christian mission is the joyous truth that Christ carries us through the agony of our suffering, all the way into the new life of the resurrection.

Alfonse was a student from Rwanda at a seminary in France where I taught. Our families worshipped and occasionally played together. Before coming to France, Alfonse and Thacienne chose to live in a slum area of the capital city of Rwanda, where Alfonse, an Anglican priest, worked in a Christian publishing house. Their dwelling had no running water, and normally fetching the water and returning with it balanced on one's head was "women's work." Alfonse felt this to be unfair, and rather than require that his wife carry the heavy load, he did the unthinkable and went to the well in the central square and brought back the water. He was not clever enough to balance it on his head— much of the water landed on his clothes. But his counter-cultural and awkward efforts didn't go unnoticed. Every woman in the slum wondered why he was doing this. Every man was both interested and threatened.

A delegation confronted Thacienne, demanding: "What herb do you give your husband to make him so kind?" She invited them to her dwelling, to show them the herb.

Opening the Bible, she read, "Come unto me all you who are weary and heavy laden, and I will give you rest. Take my yoke upon you and learn from me, for my yoke is easy and my burden light." Then she answered their question, "What is the herb my husband takes? The herb is Jesus. He is the one who makes my husband so kind." Within a matter of months, a church of more than 100 was meeting in Alfonse and Thacienne's home.

Little did Alfonse and Thacienne realize that their willingness to suffer for Christ, to be martyrs in their witness by bearing the inconvenience of slum life and the humiliation of carrying water, would be preparation for greater martyrdom. During the Rwandan massacres, Alfonse was hiding fellow Tutsis in the diocesan headquarters in Kigali. On the last day before Hutus evacuated the city, the militia came looking for him. This time the delegation at the door didn't innocently inquire about herbs. They dragged Alfonse, our brother in Christ, outside and brutally executed him. Thacienne and their children now live in Nairobi.

"I sought to know nothing among you but Christ Jesus, and him crucified." Christ carries our burdens. In knowing him, we are freed to bear those of others. The consequences are extraordinary, for "the world will believe by your love for one another" *(John 13:35)*. "We know love by this, that he laid down his life for us—and we ought to lay down our lives for one another" *(1 John 3:16)*.

We expect that this laying down of our life will be in dramatic, earth-shaking or at least life-shaking ways—like Alfonse and Thacienne. Usually, however, our lives are laid down in the mundane moments in which we bear one another's burdens. In so doing, we enable others to see the God who in his great kindness bears our sin and sorrow.

What burdens are you carrying that you need to see borne by Christ? Whose load can you bear, and in so doing help them see more of God's kindness—and thus know more of Christ crucified in their midst?

Consider this parable: One day a farmer went out to his field and noticed a fully grown, thoroughly wilted fig tree. Concerned about its barren branches, he rushed to his barn and returned with a bucket of manure to spread on its roots as fertilizer. The fig tree, disgusted by the horrid mixture about to be coated on him, proclaimed: "You're not about to put that mess on me!" and picking up his roots, the tree ran across the field into a neighboring orchard. The next day, that orchard's farmer noticed the new tree in its fruitless plight and attempted the same process. This time the tree ran screaming to the safety of the roadside, far removed from cruel farmers with their stinking manure. It so happens that the next day, Jesus was passing from Bethany to Jerusalem,

"And seeing a fig tree by the side of the road, he went to it and found nothing at all on it but leaves. Then he said to it, 'May no fruit ever come from you again'" *(Matt. 21:19)*! Suffering is actually central both to our walking in Christ's triumph, and to bearing the rich fruit he wills for our lives. Dare we say that in Christians' hands the manure of suffering is transferred into life-nurturing fertilizer?

Triumph over a defeated foe

Suffering, sin and Satan are neither senseless nor sovereign. All these have been defeated by Christ crucified. Now, by the Spirit of Christ, even suffering is redeemed and made to bear fruit.

We aren't the victors. Christ is! We do not win the triumph; we walk in his triumph. His victory does not protect us from suffering, but empowers us through suffering. Rather than removing pain, Christ redeems it.

Our life in mission resembles reading the history of an ancient battle. We know how it will end. We know that one day, lions and lambs will frolic together, all tears will be wiped away, all sorrows will cease and all suffering will end. We know that all injustices will be righted, and injuries healed, that every knee will bow in adoration of the Lamb who was slain. God will dwell among his people. Further, we know that one day we personally will be clothed with the righteousness and dignity of our Lord Jesus, and will dwell in the permanent home he's prepared for us.

We're players in a cosmic drama, the outcome of which we already know! We don't need to fear our opponents because we know that Christ's victory has already been won. Our opponents' power is limited to the lie. So much popular Christian literature seems to place greater emphasis on the power of darkness than of light. Our response whenever we encounter the adversary must be like that of a British preacher who awoke one night with his bed being shaken to and fro by the devil himself. Non-plussed, the pastor looked the devil in the eye and said, "Oh, it is only you," and rolled over to return to sleep.

Simon, a friend of mine who comes from the West African country of Togo, grew up in an animistic family. As a teenager, he heard a preacher proclaiming Christ's offer of eternal life. This sounded great to Simon, for the ancestors and their spirits had never offered anything like that. So Simon returned to his home, took off his ancestral ring meant to protect him from evil spirits, gave his life to Jesus, and waited for the spirits to come and kill him for his treason so that he could go have eternal life with our Lord.

To Simon's disappointment, the spirits failed. He didn't die! The next morning, Simon bought the three most taboo foods in his tribe, returned to his family compound and, before his family's shocked eyes, prepared what he assumed would be his last meal. He recounted to me many stories of people who'd eaten just one of these foods and gone insane, become seriously ill or mysteriously died. Simon hoped he would overdose with this suicidal soup. To his and his entire family's surprise, he lived! Now Simon faced a far more complicated task than dying to be with Christ: learning how to live for Christ and walk with Christ. By God's grace he has succeeded and is one of the most joyous, radiant witnesses for Christ I know.

If our theology is true, we can live with the relief of knowing our enemies are disarmed *(Col. 2:15)*. They still carouse, hurling about deceitful accusations. They still puff themselves up trying to convince us that our lives can really be threatened. They hungrily prowl about, seeking to devour whatever lies in their path. But we know that because of Christ, their power is limited and the damage they can inflict is only temporary, for Christ's triumph is sure.

When we live boldly in the face of what, for all appearances' sake, looks like life-threatening dangers, we manifest the triumph of Christ and march in Christ's public display of the defeat of all that seeks to diminish the life and wholeness of God's people *(2 Cor. 2:14)*.

Whom can you pray for, that they might be strengthened and encouraged by Christ, and walk in his triumph in the face of their foes?

Jim and Ann Owens, two members of our congregation, repeatedly took off for places of deepest conflict in order to manifest the light of the kingdom. Taking leave from his job as medical director at a juvenile detention facility, where his loving life magnetically drew hardened boys to himself, Jim served with Ann in refugee camps in Beirut, Somalia, Thailand and Cambodia. The utterly ordinary ways they engaged in extraordinary ministries, refusing to be daunted by darkness and suffering, encouraged hundreds of others in our congregation to say, "If God can use them like that, maybe he could even use me!" Not only did many go overseas, but our congregation launched into a dynamic refugee resettlement ministry, including a full-time language learning center, legal aid, vocational training and sponsorship of more than 100 refugee families, not to mention the establishment of a Cambodian church.

Seeing the passion of Christ in the pain of the world empassions us to take on some of that pain and thus embody the victory he has won. We are set free to live with compassion.

While visiting a leprosy hospital in India, I was asked to serve communion at the hospital chapel. One man, whose body had been hideously disfigured by the disease, had no fingers to hold the elements, so I placed the small cup on his bandaged hand where surgeons were attempting to restore use of his fingers. I placed the morsel of bread on the stump of his other hand. As he lifted them to his mouth, tears filled both our eyes. The very places where the bread and wine rested were where the hands of our Lord had been pierced— the broken body and shed blood of Christ, giving precious life to this man's ravaged body.

Afterward, he told me his story. When he contracted leprosy, his family and friends drove him out of his home and village. Fleeing for his life, he came to this Christian leprosy hospital, where under the staff's compassionate, skilled care, the disease had been arrested, his body was being restored, and his soul had been healed. When everyone else in his life told him, "Go! There is no place for you here!" only Christ and his Christians said, "Come! We've prepared a place for you!"

Mahatma Gandhi was once asked, "What would it take for India to become Christian?" He replied, "All it would take is for Christians to be Christian!" What a privilege to participate in God's marvelous love affair!

This church in India was called "The Church of Jesus Christ for Lepers." I think that's a fitting name for all churches. We all feel as if our lives are disfigured and unacceptable. To whom is God sending you as a church, inviting them to come home where places have been prepared for them? What would it take for your church to prepare to receive such "lepers"?

Tangible Hope for
Today and Eternity

6

6

Tangible Hope for Today and Eternity

In this chapter, we will look at:

- *How to fulfill our role without being driven by tasks*

- *How to balance our response to pressing local needs and urgent, more distant global needs*

- *Six ways to ensure mission remains our participation in a joyous love affair, and doesn't degenerate into a grim duty*

- *Outlining a comprehensive mission strategy for your church*

In this study, we've explored five keys to a biblical approach to mission:

1. Remembering whose mission it is.
2. Allowing our engagement in mission to be integrated around the biblical theme of the kingdom of God.
3. Understanding God and his authority in the world.
4. Participating in God's comprehensive concern for all of life.
5. Celebrating our role in fulfilling God's mission in the world.

Now we need to explore specifics of how we live out this role. This concluding chapter outlines a six-point strategy for expressing tangible, lasting hope in the midst of complex local and global needs.

Keeping our focus

In spite of the fact that our lives already seem too full and too busy, it's easy for questions such as the following to dominate any study of mission:

- Are we doing enough?

- Are we sacrificing enough?

- Are we committed enough?

- Are we focused enough?

- Are we fruitful enough?

Our "to-do" lists are saturated. We can't handle adding one more responsibility.

Yet heeding God's call to mission inescapably means we are called to do things. *We . . . are called . . . to do things.* All three parts of this sentence tempt us to return discussion of mission to a human-centered focus. Then we add a fourth dimension—urgency. Paul tells us in Colossians 4:5 to "make the most of the time," literally, to "redeem the time." This can tempt us to a heightened sense of pressure. Time seems so short. We're called as Christians not only to *save* time but to *redeem* it! How do we preserve ourselves and our church from a dis-integrating feverish round of frenetic busy-ness?

To clarify this, and to review themes discussed throughout our study, let's consider six qualities of a congregation's involvement in mission. By engaging in "quality checks" of your own as well as your church's participation in God's mission, and by orienting its mission involvement according to these qualities, you can help your congregation "make the most of every opportunity" and participate in God's redemption of time. Whether you are studying this with a group as you seek God's will for your congregation, or on your own as you seek God's will for your own life, these qualities are vital for our life-giving participation in God's mission.

For us as individuals, and for the whole church to participate in God's restoration of a whole world, our mission involvement needs to be:

1. Relational
2. Reciprocal
3. Royal
4. Radical
5. Realistic
6. Resourceful

1. Relational

Involve people in loving the Lord

We must not call ourselves or others to commitment to a task—world evangelization, reaching the unreached, restoring the inner cities, peacemaking or feeding the hungry.

We are called to a Person. Jesus Christ is our Life. If we see mission as a commitment to a task, it enters into rivalry with all the other tasks clamoring for our attention. It seems optional. If it is commitment to a Person, the Lord Jesus Christ, then it is anything but optional. Our life and the life of the world depends upon it.

Tasks are inherently in need of resources, to be dredged up or recruited. But the Lord of Creation possesses obviously unlimited resources. We do people a grave disservice if we ask them to commit to the "task of . . .". Rather we can say, "As an expression of your relationship with Christ, do you think he might be calling you to play a part in his ministry of . . ."?

Therefore, the best mission education class you can offer people is a Bible study—an opportunity to more fully understand God's heart. The goal of all mission activity is that people would more fully know God's love for them, and find themselves more in love with him as a consequence of their involvement.

Could we say this is the uniform consensus of those who have served on our mission committees and congregational boards? Are they more in love with God and with God's people because of their time on our mission committee? If not, something's wrong.

Involve people in loving people

Recognizing the danger of being repetitious, I'd like to reiterate that Jesus did not die for our programs, regardless of how wonderful they may be. The world will not believe through mission programs.

Please, when someone asks you to describe your congregation's mission "program," *remain speechless*! We shouldn't have mission programs. Rather, we need people who recognize that they are participating in God's mission. The world will believe through people who love other people as expressions of their love for God.

We often expend energy on budgets and program bureaucracies, neglecting—and even misusing—people. Too often, mission people insist on a "grin and bear it" mentality.

How many missionaries and their children have been spiritually beaten into silence by the reminder, "We must make sacrifices in the service of the Lord"? Let's make sure it is the Lord we are serving—not programs and ambitions.

Paul exhorts us to bear with one another in compassion, kindness, humility, gentleness and patience *(Col. 3:12-13)*. Yet many of us in mission actually alienate people wherever we go. People inadvertently find themselves feeling inadequate, uncommitted, unspiritual. They ask themselves, "Why am I not more . . . ?"

Another pastor on the church staff said to me one day, "Tim, every time I see you, even before you open your mouth, I feel guilty." A similar sentiment came from an elder of my congregation: "Why is it that every time you talk I feel like you are disappointed with us, and even maybe a little angry?" Where was God's grace, the essence of the gospel, the Good News?

Those concerned with mission must be the advocates of every other aspect of the life of the church. Effective mission involvement depends on good Christian education training, vibrant worship, caring fellowship groups, even a building which can be a base for launching out. Relationships between members of my own congregation's mission committee and other church committees changed dramatically when we started praying in our meetings for the other committees, and conscientiously started learning about their concerns and how we could support and encourage them. We began to function as one another's allies and advocates, rather than as opponents and accusers.

Further, if mission is concerned with crossing frontiers, bridging barriers to bring people to Christ and his kingdom, then our congregations must be places where these barriers are bridged. We mock the body of Christ if we seek to build bridges with ethnic churches in other countries, while ignoring those in our own community. The lack of distinction between Greek and Jew, barbarian and Scythian, slave and free, male and female—for Christ is all and is in all—must dominate and define our congregation's life. Without this, we will lack integrity in our mission activities.

Quality Checkpoint 1: Relational

1. Examine your recruiting and motivation efforts. To what extent do you focus on a task and to what extent on calling people to live more fully in Christ, sharing in his concerns?

2. Are you more in love with God and God's people because of your mission involvement? What would others who've been involved with you say of their own lives?

3. If someone asked for a description of your church's mission program, who are some people you'd describe?

4. To what extent are your friendships, and your church's friendships, multicultural? To whom might God be calling you to enrich the relational tapestry of your life?

2. Reciprocal

We are freed to be allies not only with people in our own congregation, but also within the world church. The majority of Christians today are non-Western. We used to speak of the Third World, and then of the Two-Thirds World (in reference to the portion of the world's population living in poverty, in the so-called "developing world"). By the year 2005, it will be the Four-Fifths World. Because the kingdom of God is a web of relationships, and because relationships are inherently bilateral, mutual and reciprocal, we are freed to be partners in mission with the global church.

So the question we need to ask is not, "How can we expand our mission program by sending more of our members as missionaries?" The question should be, "What is God doing in the world in which he's calling us to participate, and with whom can we *partner* so as to manifest signs of the coming kingdom?" The word "partner" comes from *parcener*, which meant "co-heir." To be partners with someone is to be co-heirs of the future. That is precisely who we are in the Body of Christ—co-heirs of all God's promises. Therefore, nothing is more natural than for us to live as kingdom partners in the present. For example, World Vision has an outstanding international staff of 12,000 people working in more than 100 countries. They are deeply committed, eagerly sacrificial, highly trained Christian professionals. Only a tiny percentage, however, are Westerners. The global church and the global Christian movement are indeed just that—global!

Visiting a church in Kenya a few years ago, I was impressed that the Presbyterian Church of East Africa was devoting its harvest offering that year to pay the salary of a Scottish pastor working in an inner-city parish in Edinburgh. Here was the "daughter church" giving out of its poverty to aid the "mother church."

To avoid any hint of imperialism, we must consciously admit before our brothers and sisters elsewhere that we need to be receivers and not just senders, students and not just teachers. I fear the continued growth of American missionary triumphalist imperialism, in which we inadvertently dominate the world church because we're committed, affluent and have the pragmatic temperament of pioneers willing to overcome all problems.

Unquestionably, one of the greatest gifts we can share in the Two-Thirds World (or Four-Fifths World) is the affirmation of our brothers' and sisters' worth by demonstrating our recognition that they have something to give and share. One small step would be to eliminate our term "mission field," admitting that every place is a field requiring the missionary activity of our Lord.

Another more difficult step is receiving in Christ the capacity to genuinely embrace these brothers and sisters. One of my dearest friends is a Chadian teacher who admitted that although he'd worked with missionaries for 20 years, he'd never once had one treat him as a brother. He'd enjoyed relationships with missionaries as co-workers, employer, employee, supervisor, supervisee, teacher and student—but never as friends! Crucial to overcoming this is our willingness to admit our inadequacy and need. It is fundamentally dehumanizing always to be a "helpee." We all need to be a helper. Part of our ministry is to help others discover that by God's grace they are not incompetent, that they have something worth knowing and abilities worth sharing. This mutually builds our sense of confidence, worth, trust and respect. We are freed to be partners in provoking one another to love and good works.

This will only be effective if we've addressed our own and our congregation's egotism. Only recognizing that I have died and my life is hidden in Christ who is my life *(Col. 3:3-4)* will liberate me from my addiction to be in control, to be in charge, to be appreciated and to have my name written on the fruits of a ministry. Only this will free me from requiring that things be done my way. Only then am I delivered from the pursuit of status and significance, and set free to live as a servant.

Quality Checkpoint 2: Reciprocal

1. What would it mean for you to develop genuine partnerships with non-Western Christians?

2. What do you think you need to learn and receive from Christians from other parts of the world?

3. How can we ensure high quality in our mission activities without insisting that we be in control?

3. Royal

To engage in mission is to participate in the coming of the kingdom of God. To participate in the King's business. We have a royal commission, with all the consequent significance and stature.

Without this integrating vision, mission involvement can degenerate into competition between programs, ambitions and desires. Our direction in mission can be swayed by the compelling influence and appeals of other people. In many congregations, mission activities are dominated by the interests of a few. Friends and nephews, pet projects and interests of persuasive members are brought before mission committees, and they become the objects of mission support.

When the King and his kingdom are the unifying, controlling source and goal of all we do, then competing calls and opposing ambitions fade under the sound of the King's marching orders.

Earlier, I described the kingdom of God as his redemptive totalitarianism. It is the restoration of God's reign over *all* his creation. No aspect of life remains outside God's sovereign Kingship. Therefore, the church's sphere of missionary concern extends to the whole of life and to the whole world. This is so important that it deserves some review and further elaboration.

Whole life

God proclaimed through Jeremiah, "For surely I know the plans I have for you, says the Lord, plans for your welfare and not for harm, to give you a future with hope" *(29:11)*. The King seeks to restore the well-being and wholeness of his creation. Sadly, instead of bringing God's reign to bear on the whole of life, to make lives whole, the church often wavers between being preoccupied with ghosts or corpses, rather than with people. Soul-saving churches engaging only in evangelism, seeking to convert souls while leaving the rest of people's lives unchanged, are really only relating to ghosts, for a ghost is a soul without a body. Churches participating passionately in the pursuit of social justice and welfare, unwilling to call people to repentant faith in Jesus Christ, are really only caring for corpses, for a corpse is a body without a soul. Both make a mockery of the gospel of God's kingdom and his reign over bodies and souls, now and forevermore.

The church is not an underground railway to heaven, hiding people on earth until they can escape to glory. Nor is the church another philanthropic organization, kindly doing good works and dispensing aid to those in need. Rather, the church is the body of Christ, consciously and explicitly participating in the establishment of his reign on earth. The church is to be consciously and explicitly Christ's, regardless of the activity. On my first day in my first ministry after being ordained, I received a welcoming visit from a Tlingit Indian woman. Mrs. Karras arrived with a plate of cookies and a word of advice: "Tim, whatever you do here among us, please lift Jesus up, for he said, 'If I be lifted up, I will draw all people to myself.'"

Therefore, as mentioned earlier, we extend both hands of the gospel: the hand inviting people to repentance, faith and eternal reconciliation with God through Christ Jesus, and the hand manifesting deeds of mercy and compassion, extending the goodness of God's kingdom on earth. One is not a means to the other. Both are equally significant to life in the eternal kingdom as described by Scripture.

Whole world

In his last sermon, Jesus described four spheres in which we are to be witnesses to his kingdom: Jerusalem, Judea, Samaria and the ends of the earth *(Acts 1:1-10)*. Churches often interpret this command as something we must complete sequentially. First we take care of our needs at home, then we move out toward the ends of the earth. Reacting against this, other churches respond to the call to the farthest corners of the world, and skip over their Samaria. I believe we are called and empowered by the Spirit to be witnesses in all four spheres—simultaneously, not sequentially! Two of these are unavoidable, two are avoidable.

The unavoidable world

- Our community (Jerusalem)

- Our country (Judea)

The avoidable world

- People of differing cultural backgrounds than our own who live around us (Samaria)

- The ends of the earth

We can't avoid certain relationships in our own community and country. Intentionally or not, we are inevitably witnesses among the people with whom we live and work. But there are people we can avoid, either because of cultural differences or geographic distance.

Jesus implies that every church is to engage in some form of ministry in each of these four spheres!

This truth was brought home to me through a visit in Bangalore, India. My congregation sent me to learn from Vinay Samuel and the dynamic ministry of St. John's Church and other area churches among the poor and destitute in the Bangalore slums. After several days of demonstrating the quality of care and extent of change the people of these churches were enabling, Vinay asked me as we walked through an oppressive neighborhood, "Tim, what is your church doing for the poor in Seattle?"

The compelling integrity of Vinay and Colleen Samuel's life gave force to his question. One Sunday in their slum church, a notorious prostitute—she was the "madame" who controlled prostitution in the entire region, and nominally a Muslim— entered their church. Colleen immediately walked over to her, put her arm around her and unquestioningly welcomed her to worship. She became a regular at their services and Bible studies and, after a few months, gave her life to Christ. Colleen continued to nurture her in her new faith and one day, the woman announced to Vinay that she wanted to be baptized. For Vinay to have baptized a famous Muslim woman could potentially have provoked a major religious riot. Wisely, he went to the local Muslim leader, told him of this woman's decision to follow Christ and her desire for baptism, and boldly invited him to try for a month to discourage her.

Just three days later, the Muslim leader returned to Vinay and said, "It's no use. She's determined to follow Jesus."

Vinay then said, "You know our custom regarding baptism. Do I have your permission to baptize her?"

He replied, "Go ahead and do what you must." The next day, Vinay publicly baptized this new sister. She went on to become one of the region's leading evangelists!

Thus, Vinay's question about what our church was doing for the poor in our own community was a divinely directed arrow. We were financially supporting various ministries in our community, but the people of our church were either focused on our own Jerusalem and Judea, or being sent out to the ends of the earth. Samaritans in our midst were relationally avoided. Developing a sister church relationship with a congregation in India is commendable, but what about an ethnic church in our own town? To send a work team to reroof an orphanage in Haiti is a marvelous expression of the kingdom, but God also calls us to provide roofs over the heads of the homeless in our midst.

Quality Checkpoint 3: Royal

1. How would you evaluate your church's ministry to whole people: souls, as well as bodies and emotions? Do you tend to stress one above the other? What steps could you take to extend both hands of the gospel?

2. How are you participating in God's ministry in your
   - Jerusalem?
   - Judea?
   - Samaria?
   - the ends of the earth?

3. What next steps might God be calling you to regarding your
   - Jerusalem?
   - Judea?
   - Samaria?
   - the ends of the earth?

---

4. Radical

If our desire is to enable mission to be at the root of our congregation's life, then because we desire Jesus Christ to be our foundation, every aspect of our church's life must be infused with a burning passion for Christ and his kingdom.

Our call is to enable all people to become all God intends them to be. We want to help them experience the joyous delight of seeing God use them in the coming of his kingdom. We want, therefore, to enable everyone in our congregation to experience—not merely be the receptacles of information about—involvement in Christ's mission.

St. Francis is reputed to have replied to a request that he go talk with the Holy Roman Emperor by saying, "There was a time when I too believed in words." He was not cynical about the power of words; after all, he eventually went to talk with the Muslim sultanate, seeking an end to the Crusades. Rather, Francis expressed the truth that life, not mere talk, speaks loudest.

A recent survey examined the most compelling motivating factor in people's decision to become involved in mission service. Here are the findings:

- 5 percent replied, "the Bible";

- 10 percent said, "the needs of the world";

- 40 percent answered, "personal exposure to mission"; and

- 45 percent said, "personal relationships with missionaries, national Christians and people in need."

When our Lord said, "Where your treasure is your heart will be also," he was obviously referring to money. But for many in the Western world today, our greatest treasure is not money but time. Therefore, if we want people's hearts engaged with God's heart in mission, we must enable their time to be invested there.

This presents a challenge, for most people's schedules are already too full. There are some, but not many, who are looking for something to do. Most need to find ways of making their current engagements more meaningful, or else be liberated to invest their time in other ways. We must begin with people's existing time commitments, instead of asking them to add some new activity to their lives. We must move mission to where people are, rather than ask people to come to mission activities.

Our mission committee had great fun brainstorming how to make people's current church activities more mission-focused. We thought of ways the worship services, Sunday school classes and small group fellowships could allow moments of mission experience. Our brainstorming produced a range of ideas, including more specific global prayers; fellowship groups meeting missionaries, refugees, or international students, and developing "sister" relationships with similar groups in other churches; Sunday schools visiting local ministries or other ethnic churches during normal class sessions.

One year our congregation's mission conference did not include any extra meetings. We actually called it the "Mission Unconference." During a four-week period, we brought to most of the fellowship groups, coffee hours and worship services (more than 250 different groups and activities) mission activities enabling people to taste the delight of participating in our Lord's coming kingdom. It took an entire year to organize. But never again could our people say they hadn't been exposed to stimulating and exciting presentations of what God was doing around the world.

The congregation even developed an extensive program for maximizing people's vacations, called "Vacation with a Purpose." People go on vacation. Why not enable them to experience a vacation where they can actually participate in some dimension of mission? Mission is no longer the domain of a few eccentrics and fanatics in our church. Mission is not just the activity of a few specialists, but the passion of the people of God who allow their hearts to beat in harmony with God's heart.

At University Presbyterian Church in Seattle, we were deceived when 500 people attended a mission activity. When we realized that number represented only 15 percent of the congregation, we knew something was wrong. University Presbyterian isn't the exception. Most congregations can expect 10 to 15 percent to attend a mission event. That's wonderful—but how do you bring mission education to the other 85 percent? One way is to not expect people to add new commitments but to find creative ways to carve minutes out of existing programs.

Quality Checkpoint 4: Radical

What can be done to deepen people's passion to participate in God's mission? Analyze existing church activities and see how you can weave mission education into those programs. What can you do in each allotted time, gradually expanding time commitments when possible? Use the chart on the following page to record your ideas.

	5 minutes	15 minutes	1 hour	3 hours over several weeks
Sunday School				
Adult Education				
Small Groups				
Committees				
Worship				

5. Realistic

Having read all this, you might easily be feeling exhausted and oppressed. This study began by noting how easily mission involvement becomes burdensome when we approach it as a human-centered activity, and when we motivate people by pinpointing all they are not doing that they could and should do. We need constant reminders that we are but human participants in divine actions, empowered and equipped with God's resources. Instead of listening to someone else's list of what we should be doing, we must seek the King and hear how he would have us—individuals and congregations—participate in the coming of his kingdom.

If we attempt too many things at once, we'll quickly feel like firefighters battling towering blazes with teaspoons. But if we focus rather than dabble, what would it take for us to concur with Paul when he said in 2 Timothy 4:5, "Complete the ministry which has been given to you"? Would we know when we've completed something? To say "yes" to the right things, we must make sure we are also saying "no" to the right things.

Does God call churches to focus on a few things and do them well, or to skim the surface trying to cover as much ground as possible? Merely to say, "We are supporting 125 missionaries" is commendable, but meaningless. The real question is how well do you support them? This requires us to focus our actions.

Focus on a few people

Begin by focusing on those in your congregation who are interested in mission. Study and pray with them. Do things together in mission in your own community. Meet with national leaders and missionaries as they come to town. Most missionaries agree they'd prefer to meet for an evening with a living room full of people who are excited about mission than with a church hall full of the unconvinced.

Passion for mission is personal, and spreads personally. Enable a few to grow in their enthusiasm, and soon a larger group will be infected. We all know that our Lord focused on 12 disciples to prepare a people to reach the world. Yet in our mass-oriented society, it's easy to be sidetracked into pursuing bigger numbers. A few individuals, thoroughly infected with the Lord's passion for his creation, can joyously spread the "condition" to the entire body.

Next, focus on interests in which some people are already involved, and allow those to be springboards to additional ways of participating in God's mission.

Focus on knowing a few missionaries well, rather than maintaining a casual, financially-driven involvement with many. The goal is relationship, not finances or numbers. Remember, people—not programs—are our passion. Find missionaries and non-Western Christian leaders with whom people can relate, and that seek a reciprocal relationship with those in your congregation. Then provide and promote opportunities for relationships to develop through correspondence, gift exchanges, visits, etc. Relationships develop over time, so don't allow ambitions or urgency to dictate the process. Dynamic involvement will grow out of a strong relationship.

Once relationship is established, the practical and financial matters can be fleshed out. When a commitment is made, it should be kept. Cardinal rules for supporting missionaries are:

- "Thou Shalt Know Thy Missionaries"

- "To Know Thee is to Love Thee"

- "Do Unto Thy Missionaries as Thou Wouldst be Done Unto." And remember, love never fails.

Obviously, this is most influential when a congregation has the privilege of sending "its own." When Jim and Ann Owens from our congregation went to work in a refugee camp in Thailand, overnight the entire church's interest and concern was riveted on Cambodian refugees. When Denny and Jeanne Grindall started building irrigation systems among the Maasai of East Africa, everyone became interested in Kenya. The Lord's raising up of people from the midst of our congregations should be a focus of our prayer and involvement. Nothing will be more effective at moving mission to the core of our church's life.

Focus on a few key local ministries

When asked, "What is your church doing for the poor in your city?" our own integrity as Christians in mission requires that we offer a clear response. This is not merely a matter of pointing to where our church's budget is allocated, but to where our congregation's members are involved.

Build bridges to global ministries

Let's review several ways in which bridges can be built between groups in a congregation and ministries around the world:

- Small group fellowships can be given the names of one missionary or national church leader, one country, one unreached people group or local ministry for which they can pray. These become ideal groups to host visitors from that area and to pass on information and news, as well as requests for assistance.

- Short-term mission education opportunities are abundant, and are vital components of a congregation's portfolio of mission possibilities.

- Youth groups can engage in service projects, locally or in other countries. These can open eyes and affirm the worth and significance both of group members and of those with whom they work hand-in-hand.

- Multi-generational skilled mission teams can be sent to areas with corresponding needs for those skills.

- Sister-church relationships are indispensable in expanding a congregation's horizons.

Build relationships with people in each community, and not just with a missionary. Missionaries eventually leave, and we want bridges that will last forever.

Quality Checkpoint 5: Realistic

1. Who are missionaries and non-Western Christian leaders you know? If you know none, how might you build these relationships? What tangible steps could you take to care for them?

2. How would your average member answer this question: What is your church doing for the poor in your community? How can you deepen the focus and heighten awareness of and involvement in your church's local ministries?

3. What global partnerships do you have, or might be natural for you to develop? How can you more fully extend these so everyone in your congregation participates in them?

6. Resourceful

Mission isn't a human enterprise, dependent on our own finite plans and provisions. We are participating in the King of Creation's concerns. We are citizens in God's kingdom. We must fully avail ourselves of resources he provides.

Supernatural resources

To remind us of the obvious, engaging in mission is participating in a spiritual battle. We do not labor against flesh and blood. Therefore we do not labor only with flesh and blood. Through years of service, I've come to realize that perhaps one of the most valuable things I do as a missionary is serve as a conduit of people's prayer for a particular part of the world—drawing other Christians' attention to the conflict between the kingdoms of light and darkness in that region. In all probability, most would not be praying for that region with the same interest if they'd not known me.

As is to be expected, when our daughters worked in Siberia and Uganda, we prayed for those regions of God's world like never before! In fact, we feel a permanent bond. One of the great gifts of World Vision's child sponsorship program is the way it focuses people's care and prayer on a specific person in a specific place. It's hard to pray meaningfully for raw statistics. A face, a name, a place can be brought before the Lord with passion and conviction.

Fundamental to any ministry is the provision of specific prayer requests for God's prayer warriors. This is not preparation for the battle, it is the battle. This is not a means to get the necessary resources, it is our primary resource.

Prayer, fasting and Scripture study are vital to develop spiritual disciplines that are indispensable resources for mission. I don't eat breakfast as a duty or obligation. I like to eat breakfast, and I'm grouchy by noon if I don't. So why have we made Bible study a Christian duty? Without it, we are spiritually starving ourselves and lacking resources for the long haul. Don't starve yourself! Dig in!

Material resources

Tom Sine loves to challenge groups to design innovative ministry responses to local and world needs without relying on their church's budget. We turn too quickly to the church budget as the easiest solution to material needs. He suggests we instead cultivate the skill of being "creative scroungers." Two such scroungers were Al and Jan, who decided that by selling their car and giving away the money it cost to operate it, they could fully support a ministry in Haiti. Irritating moments of running for a bus in the rain took on new meaning: each slosh through a puddle reminded them to pray for that ministry.

Our desire is obviously not merely that people would give their money. If people invest their time in mission, their hearts will follow. Therefore we speak of "whole life stewardship," calling people to be stewards of their whole lives, not just of a percentage of their finances. Don't merely tithe the fruit of your labor. Tithe the fruit of your experience—giving to others from the skills and wisdom the Lord has enabled you to gain!

In all of this, we are merely offering God access to that which is already his. We own nothing, but are stewards of all things. We don't give only what we can afford. We give out of our poverty, so that God's kingdom might abound.

Similarly, we send people we can't afford to lose, for because their lives and skills are invaluable here, they are equally valuable elsewhere.

As Paul says in 2 Corinthians 8:2-15, this kind of giving is a privilege and joy, something we beg to be able to do when we can see the fruit of our lives making a difference in the kingdom.

After years of slavery in a Muslim family in northern Chad, an elderly Christian woman returned to her home village after being freed. Not only had she given her services to the family, she had borne her master's children, and now she returned penniless and family-less. Her village church welcomed her home, building her a house, buying her a goat and giving her her first pair of sandals. As she began to rebuild her life, her church decided to send a missionary couple to proclaim the gospel among the Muslims in the north. She longed to be able to support them, but literally had no money. On the day of this couple's commissioning, she tearfully walked to the front of the church to present her offering, and laid her sandals on the table. She said, "My feet are too old and tired now to go myself, but sell my shoes so they can be used by you to carry the Good News."

"How beautiful are the feet of those who bring glad tidings of good things" *(Rom. 10:15)*!

Quality Checkpoint 6: Resourceful

1. How can you intensify the quality and focus of your own and your church's prayer for the world?

2. What would need to change in your personal stewardship, and in your church's stewardship program, to institute an emphasis on whole life stewardship ?

May God lead your beautiful feet into ever more delightful adventures of life in his kingdom. Whether your feet are old and tired, young and restless, skilled or clumsy, by the grace of God they are beautiful bearers of you—a messenger of glad tidings and good things for all nations!

Taking the Next Step

7

Taking the Next Step

7

Robert A. Seiple
World Vision President

God calls each of us on a pilgrimage of faith—and you have just walked your way through a valuable roadmap for that pilgrimage. This study was not written merely to provide us with stimulating insight. Rather, its purpose is to propel us into more fruitful involvement.

As President of World Vision for more than 10 years, I have had the privilege of seeing thousands of "beautiful feet" in dozens of countries as I have walked alongside some of the world's neediest people. These are women, men and children who are making a difference in their world as they walk the pilgrimage of faith the Lord has set before them.

There is nothing extraordinary about the feet that carry them. They come in all sizes, shapes and colors. Yet in the midst of their rich diversity, God works miracles through committed lives—lives motivated by passion and compassion.

They have a passion for God to be glorified and for others to discover the fullness of life for which we were created in Christ. They know the stakes are eternal and they have chosen to play their lives out with eternity in mind. Thus, they refuse to settle for smaller goals than the ones that count forever. Their hearts also are broken by a deep compassion. In fact, they are often grieved over the hardship and suffering of others. These are feet motivated to walk where others are unwilling to walk, to experience thorns and pains that most would avoid. They do this because the love of Christ compels them—not to a task but to lives wholly devoted to Christ. They can't help but walk, and keep on walking.

One such person is Suing, who I met recently in Vietnam. We spent four hours together. She had traveled six more hours to meet with me. Suing is 73 and her life is passionate, carried on beautiful feet. Bob Pierce, World Vision's founding president, first met Suing in 1962. She was running an orphanage with 29 children and helping her husband manage a growing church of 2,000 believers. Bob promised an ongoing commitment of $10 a month for each child to help with the orphanage expenses. In return, Suing promised she would be faithful in caring for her children.

Both determined to keep their promises. By early 1975, however, the war was lost, the Americans were gone and World Vision was forced to leave its ministry behind. In the next five years only one $10 check would reach her village. As the North Vietnamese attacked her village, Suing lost one of her own children, killed by a shell in front of their church. Suing's husband and her eldest son were taken captive. She never saw them again. Another child managed to escape, eventually coming to the United States.

Recently, more than 20 years later, this son returned for a visit. He begged his mother to move with him to the States. "It's so much easier in America," the son said. "I can take care of you. Your hardship will be over." Suing replied, "Son, you know of my promise to God and to Bob Pierce to take care of God's children here. I'm now reconciled to the fact that your father will not be coming back to finish this ministry. But when I meet him in heaven, I want to go from this place!" Suing's orphans have all grown up. Like Suing, they have stayed with the church and are its key lay leaders. That church today is pastored by this 73-year-old woman and is now a church of 19,000 believers. The church is very much alive and well, and the gates of hell will not prevail against it! Beautiful feet carry compassionate people who are propelled by passion for Christ.

Throughout this book we've had the opportunity to reprioritize and refocus our involvement in God's mission. It is not a dour duty, but an exceptional privilege. What next steps is God calling you to take? God doesn't ask us to wait for extraordinary, far-reaching, highly "noble" opportunities. He invites us to take the next step of faithful obedience. Suing's commitment to 29 children led to a church that grew 950 percent through extraordinarily difficult circumstances.

This book has provided you with rich insights into what you might do. Now, "knowing these things, blessed are you if you do them" *(John 13:17)*. As you step out on this pilgrimage, World Vision exists to partner with you. We can link you in dozens of ways with children and with community-transforming projects in one of the more than 100 countries where we work. We can help you find ways of walking with Good News in the midst of the complex needs that exist in cities throughout the U.S. May the God of mission, who has you in the world, work out through you his good, acceptable and perfect will in such a way that both you and the world will never be the same again!

To contact us at World Vision, write to:

The Institute for Global Engagement

P.O. Box 9716

Federal Way, WA 98063-9716

or call toll free: 1-888-552-1508